The ancient monuments of the Western Isles

A Visitors' Guide to the Principal Historic Sites and Monuments
Text by Noel Fojut, Denys Pringle and Bruce Walker
Edited by Denys Pringle

HISTORIC SCOTLAND

EDINBURGH: HMSO

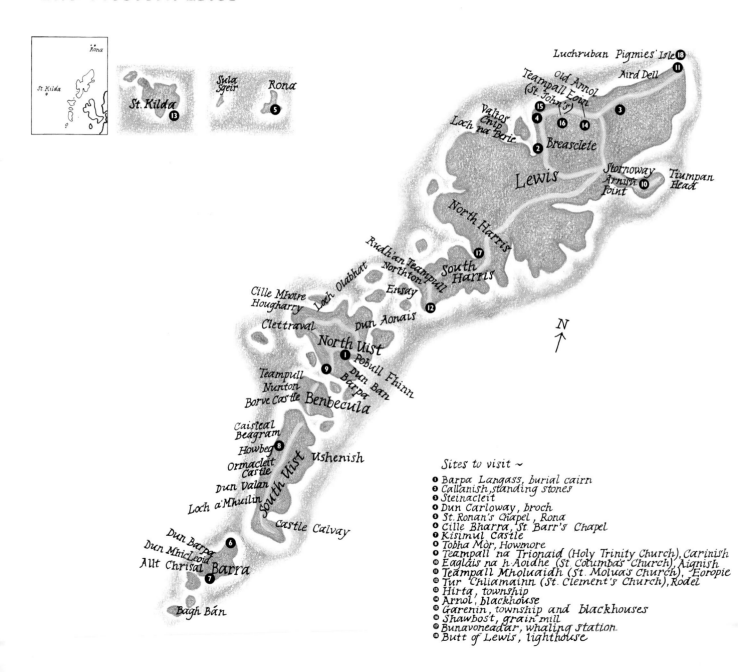

The Western Isles

Rona

St. Kilda

Rona

St. Kilda **13**

Sula Sgeir

Rona **5**

Luchruban Pigmies' Isle **18**

Old Arnol
Teampall Eoin
(St. John's)
Aird Dell
Breasclete **15**

4 **16** **14** **3**

Valtos
Cnip
Loch na Beirie

2

Breasclete

Stornoway
Arnish
Point **10**
Tiumpan
Head

Lewis

North Harris

South Harris **17**

Rudh'an Teampull
Northton

Ensay

Loch Olabhat

12

Cille Mhoire
Hougharry

Clettraval

Dun Aonais

North Uist **1**
Pobull Fhinn

9
Dun Ban
Barpa

Teampull
Nunton
Borve Castle

Benbecula

Caisteal
Beagram
Howbeg **8**
Ormacleit
Castle
Dun Valan
Loch a'Mhuilin

South Uist

Ushenish

Castle Calvay

Dun Barpa
Dun Mhicleoid
Allt Chrisal **7** Barra **6**

Bagh Bán

N

↑

Sites to visit ~

- ❶ Barpa Langass, burial cairn
- ❷ Callanish, standing stones
- ❸ Steinacleit
- ❹ Dun Carloway, broch
- ❺ St. Ronan's Chapel, Rona
- ❻ Cille Bharra, St Barr's Chapel
- ❼ Kisimul Castle
- ❽ Tobha Mòr, Howmore
- ❾ Teampall na Trionaid (Holy Trinity Church), Carinish
- ❿ Eaglais na h-Aoidhe (St Columba's Church), Aignish
- ⓫ Teampall Mholuaidh (St. Molua's Church), Eoropie
- ⓬ Tur Chliamainn (St. Clement's Church), Rodel
- ⓭ Hirta, township
- ⓮ Arnol, blackhouse
- ⓯ Garenin, township and blackhouses
- ⓰ Shawbost, grain mill
- ⓱ Bunavoneadar, whaling station
- ⓲ Butt of Lewis, lighthouse

Contents

Introduction

North and west of the Scottish mainland lie the Western Isles (known also as the Outer Hebrides), a chain of islands stretching 200 km north–south from the Butt of Lewis to Barra Head, with outliers such as Rona and Sula Sgeir 70 km to the north, the St Kilda group 55 km to the west, and Rockall a further 300 km out into the North Atlantic. Today, only about a dozen islands support human habitation. Yet the remains of past settlements, tombs and places of work and worship have been found on over fifty, many of them no more than dots on the map.

This guidebook looks at the archaeological and architectural heritage of the islands, concentrating on some of the best–preserved sites and monuments that can be visited by the public.

Although every attempt has been made to ensure that the details concerning access to the 'Sites to Visit' are correct at the time of going to press, visitors should always check locally and ask permission before crossing crofting land. No right of access may be assumed for any of the other sites mentioned in this book.

The islands of Lewis and Harris, North Uist, Benbecula, South Uist, Barra, and their numerous attendants are formed from some of the world's oldest rocks. But despite this primeval ancestry, much of the landscape of the Western Isles is relatively recent, and is still changing.

Along the west coast are long beaches of shell-sand interrupted by bold cliffed head-lands. The beaches are backed by spreads of windblown sand, forming gently sloping fertile lands, known as the 'machair'. Low rocky hills blanketed in peat stretch across the islands to their rugged eastern shores.

To understand the history of settlement in the Western Isles it is necessary to know that the beach, machair and peat areas are not fixed. Remains of settlements from the Neolithic, Bronze Age and Iron Age, established originally well behind the dunes, but then buried by the encroaching sand, emerge from time to time as erosion rolls over them; for a brief while they stand crumbling on the shore before being swept away for ever. Even quite recent settlement sites are now succumbing to the sea: for example, Old

Arnol (Lewis), which was abandoned in favour of the present village in the eighteenth century. Inland, with higher hills and boggy hollows, most of the land only acquired its present extensive blanket of peat long after mankind appeared in the Isles; this too conceals remains of past farming landscapes and settlements.

What then was the landscape like, some six thousand years ago, before human settlement and the growth of the peat? Alòng the west coast would have stretched dunes, and behind them deep sandy soils with extensive scrub woodland and reedy pools. Inland from this was an area of rolling boggy ground; bare outcrops, partly covered by damp heavy soils and supporting more scrub, would have been interspersed with open areas of grassland and deep lochs and lochans fringed with reeds, formed in hollows left by the ice. Along the east coast, beyond the bare hilltops, deep sea lochs gave

Machair lying over bedrock - Barra

access into a tangle of low hills, and small but deep, wooded valleys. From the rivers salmon and trout made their way into the lochs. It was a rich land, such as Celtic mythology describes as Tir nan Og, the Land of the Ever-Young.

The Mesolithic and Early Neolithic periods: explorers, exploiters and settlers (c.7000–c.3600 BC)

The first inhabitants of Scotland after the Ice Age were hunter-gatherers, who moved along the coasts and up the river valleys, living off the land, the rivers and the sea. These Mesolithic (or Middle Stone Age) people, had a systematically ordered economic system. Each spring, family groups would move out from homes near the shore, taking with them the last of the supplies of dried meat and fish that had seen them through the winter. Living off shoots, buds and young plants, and fishing as they went, they kept on the move throughout spring, summer and autumn, going from one traditional camp site to another, hunting deer, collecting eggs or fledglings off sea cliffs, and harvesting wild fruits, especially hazelnuts. Wild food was everywhere: fungi, bark, grasses, herbs, leaves, virtually any living thing. The small number of people and their method of exploiting these natural resources were such that they did not at first place any great strain on the environment. Each year, the seasons repaired their inroads.

Gradually, however, numbers would have built up, new groups would have been formed, and parties would have set out to find new territory where all the varied needs of life were available. By this process, small communities gradually became established all the way around the Scottish coast and islands. Jura and Rum, in the Inner Hebrides, have some of the best, and earliest, evidence for Mesolithic settlers. Although there is no archaeological evidence for the settlement of Mesolithic people in the Western Isles, it seems likely that they would have reached Lewis, Harris or the Uists. But almost the entire length of the west coast, where we should expect their settlements to have been, has been removed since Mesolithic times by the rising sea level.

In areas such as the Western Isles where nature is so influential in all aspects of human life, it is often hard to separate the various strands of human economies. To the present day, the men of Ness go out annually to Sula Sgeir, a rock in the open ocean, to kill and preserve young gannets (gugas), in a distant echo of Mesolithic seasonal harvesting practice. The simple distinction between hunter-gatherer and farmer has never really applied to the Atlantic fringes of Scotland.

The Neolithic and Bronze Age: cairns and circles (c.3600–c.500 BC)

Traces of the farms of the earliest agriculturalists in the Western Isles are elusive. A few sites are known, but most of them appear to date from many centuries after farming became established in Scotland around 3600 BC. In the Western Isles, the change to farming was probably initiated by immigrants from the mainland.

Apart from burial cairns and standing stones, very few sites or monuments dating before the Iron Age give us any clear insights into the domestic life of those who created them. Some settlements have been revealed by excavation, but few of them exhibit upstanding remains to interest the visitor.

Settlement sites dating to the Neolithic and Bronze Age have been excavated, however, at Northton (Harris), Loch Olabhat (North Uist) and Allt Chrisal (Barra). At these sites small oval stone-built houses were found to be associated with an abundance of broken pottery and midden material – domestic refuse that was accumulated and allowed to rot down before being spread on the fields. Several other sites near Northton, and some fragments of field walling and possible oval houses appearing at Aird Dell and

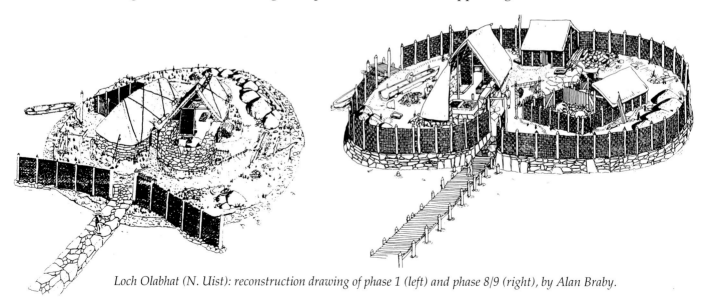

Loch Olabhat (N. Uist): reconstruction drawing of phase 1 (left) and phase 8/9 (right), by Alan Braby.

elsewhere in Lewis, suggest that there was reasonably extensive settlement in the coastal zone and on the land behind it. Recent excavations near the burial cairn of Barpa Carinish (North Uist) have revealed walls, perhaps of fields, beneath the peat, as well as hearths and scatters of pottery. It seems likely that a great deal of evidence of agricultural settlements lies under peat throughout the Isles. Unlike the great cairns and the standing stones, however, the slighter walls of ruined houses and fields would eventually have been buried completely by the peat, which grew up over most of the area in the years following 1500 BC. By the early years of the Christian era most of the landscape was as we see it today: a barren, heather- or grass-covered moorland.

It requires a great stretch of the imagination to re-create the pre-peat landscape and the farming life that it supported. Possibly it would have been not unlike the poorer parts of Aberdeenshire at the turn of the present century, with extensive grazing lands of poorer quality studded with outcrops of rock and glacial boulders. Here and there small pockets of deeper soil, cleared of stones and laboriously fertilised with seaweed, sea-sand and manure, would have supported crops of barley and even wheat; oats was not introduced until the Iron Age. But the economy, although mixed, must always have been strongly pastoral, with cattle and sheep ranging across the land. It is not known whether prehistoric field walls were intended to enclose or exclude animals, or simply to denote ownership. It may be that, as in later times, animals were herded away from the cropland during the summer growing season. Throughout prehistory and on into the Middle Ages, the contribution of wild resources, such as red deer, seals, seabirds and other wildfowl, fish, shellfish and seaweed, would have been a considerable support to the economy.

The principal monuments of the early Neolithic period, when farming became established, are communal burial

Aird Dell (Lewis), walling exposed below peat.

mounds, known as chambered cairns, and the great stone alignments and circles, for which Lewis is so well known.

Although excavations at the cairns of Uneval and Clettraval (North Uist) have established that these great mounds of stone served as burial places, many questions remain to be answered. For example, why are the cairns so noticeably concentrated in certain areas, particularly North Uist? We know that some cairns were used over several centuries, but how often were they cleared out and refurbished? Did everyone in the community eventually receive burial in a cairn, or was that accorded only to some? And if so, what were the criteria for selection? Finally, what was it, after centuries of use, that determined when a cairn was done with as a burial place? For many have been found sealed up, but by no means full.

It is easy to see why cairns have so fascinated archaeologists. What does seem to be clear, to judge from the considerable effort that must have gone into building them, is that they would have played an important part in the social and spiritual life of the people who built them.

With so many questions to be answered, there is much work for archaeologists still to do. In fact, few chambered cairns in the Western Isles have been excavated at all competently to modern standards. Thus, while we know that human bones were often buried in them along with pottery vessels, we know very little about the disposition of the bodies and artefacts within the tomb chambers; and many of our ideas about them are based on work carried out on burial cairns outside these islands. In many cases all that we have to go on are the structural remains of the cairn itself, for most of the cairns in the Western Isles have been dug into at various times. At Clettraval and Uneval, Iron Age houses were built into them, and we know that it was a regular Viking hobby to dig into 'howes' in search of treasure.

There are many cairns throughout the Western Isles. Some of the most massive, such as Dun Bharpa (Barra), may be undisturbed, and are now protected for future investigation. However, a good idea of the layout of the most common type, known as the 'passage grave', may be gained by examining a readily accessible example at Barpa Langass (North Uist), which is the only chambered cairn in the Western Isles known to

retain its original roofed chamber and passage intact (see page 13).

Such cairns appear to have been constructed in stages. First the chamber and passage were built, then a small circular cairn around the chamber, just large enough to support the thrust of the corbelled roofing, which often rests on the cairn material rather than on the chamber walls. Then would come the kerb, and sometimes a façade; and finally the space between the small cairn and the kerb would be filled in and the original small cairn buried as the mound rose higher. In certain cases, the façade would be built last of all, after the cairn had been completed, and possibly even after burials had ceased. Once a cairn was built, it would have been used in ways that we can now only dimly comprehend, serving not only as a burial mausoleum, but also very possibly as a centre of worship, ritual and social gathering.

Callanish (see page 13), on the west coast of Lewis, is the centre for the standing stones and stone circles. There are others elsewhere, including the fine Pobull Fhinn, south-east of Barpa Langass (North Uist), and there are many isolated standing stones; but the group of about twenty intervisible sites around Callanish represents the most varied collection of standing stones in Britain. Apart from the circle and avenue of the main complex, it includes simple circles or near-circles, arcs, alignments, and single stones. In the same area are several small chambered cairns, including one built into the main setting itself; but these do not compare in scale with the more massive cairns found elsewhere in the Western Isles.

(top) Dun Bharpa (Barra), cairn.
(middle) Bharpa Langass (N. Uist), cairn.
Pobull Fhinn (N. Uist), stone circle.

What was the significance of these great stone monuments, and why were they sited where they were? Although self-styled experts on the meaning of stone circles abound, in fact no-one knows. There is no doubt, however, that some, though not all, of the stone circles contain alignments which correlate with the positions occupied by the heavenly bodies at certain specific times of the year. The rising and setting of the sun and – particularly at Callanish – the position of the moon at the summer and winter solstices, and at the equinoxes, seem to have been particularly significant events. That such observations were made there seems little doubt; but accurate measurement would have required more precise tools than large lumps of rock. This suggests that the stone alignments and circles were intended less for the scientific observation of the heavens, than as appropriate settings in which to celebrate the principal points in the calendar, with all its implications for the growing season for crops and the fertility of the earth.

Whatever the origins and purpose of stone circles may have been, in social terms they represented considerable feats of communal effort in a society where everyday life was carried on around small stone houses of very modest construction. Like the great chambered tombs, which may largely – but not totally – pre-date them, they represent a bold statement of the capabilities of the communities who built them. Indeed, since the labour involved was not productive in economic terms, this may have been one of their purposes, to demonstrate to all comers the wealth and security of their builders, who had

either the time to spare for such extravagance or the power to command it. Although archaeologists can provide details about the physical layout of chambered cairns and stone circles, research has not taken us very far into the minds of the Neolithic farmers who built them. But perhaps that is too ambitious a goal in any case, even for modern science. Whatever their original purpose may have been, today's visitors can stand, ponder and speculate for themselves in the presence of these inspiring monuments.

Pollachar Stone (S.Uist)

Neolithic and Bronze Age sites to visit:

1. Barpa Langass burial cairn (North Uist)

Accessible by foot, 150 m S of the A867 Clachan–Lochmaddy road (NF 838657).

Barpa Langass cairn stands on a heathery hillside, overlooking Loch a'Bharpa. Its location on the side of a hill, rather than the top, is a typical one for such burial cairns. On the far side of the same hill is a well-preserved stone circle, known as Pobull Fhinn.

The cairn is circular in plan, 25 m in diameter and 4 m high. It originally had a well-defined outer kerb, formed with large boulders linked by short stretches of drystone walling. The entrance is on the east. A narrow pasage, 4 m long, opens from a concave forecourt let into the outer kerb; in contrast to the better known cairns of Orkney and elsewhere, the passage is low and long. It leads into an oval burial chamber, measuring some 4 by 1.8 m, with a high corbelled roof supported on the huge stone slabs that form the walls.

Excavation many years ago found burnt bone, an arrowhead, some flakes of flint and fragments of Bronze Age pottery – all dating perhaps from the last time that the tomb was entered in antiquity.

2. Callanish standing stones (Lewis)

Located at the south end of Callanish township, signposted from the A858 with car park near by (NB 213330). In the care of Historic Scotland.

The main site at Callanish stands on a low ridge, visible for many miles around. The plan is unique. A circle of standing stones is the terminus for a double row, or avenue, of stones leading north. To the east, south and west single rows lead off from the circle. The stones are gneiss, and are set up with their long axes aligned to the row or circle. The circle consists of thirteen stones, up to 3.5 m tall, with a central single stone over 4.7 m high. The lines of stones radiating from it are irregularly spaced, and only the southerly line is precisely aligned on its cardinal compass direction.

Until 1857, only the upper parts of the stones could be seen. In that year, however, a thick layer of peat was removed on the orders of the landowner, Sir James Matheson, and a previously

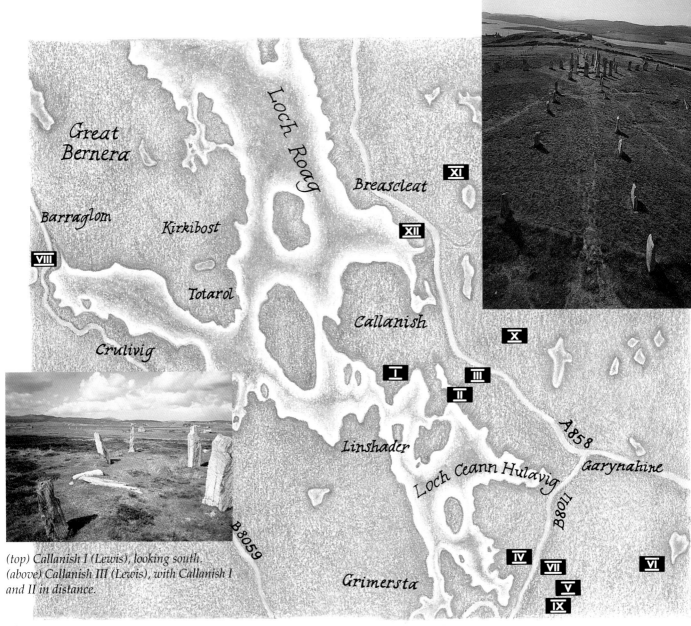

Great
Bernera

Loch Roag

Breascleat

XI

XII

Barraglom

Kirkibost

VIII

Totarol

Callanish

X

Crulivig

I

III

II

Linshader

A858

Garynahine

Loch Ceann Hulavig

B8011

B 8059

Grimersta

IV

VII

VI

V

IX

(top) Callanish I (Lewis), looking south.
(above) Callanish III (Lewis), with Callanish I
and II in distance.

Callanish II (Lewis).

unsuspected feature was revealed: the remains of a small chambered cairn within the central circle. The cairn is roofless. It incorporates two of the stones of the eastern side of the circle in its kerb, flanking the entrance to its passage, whilst the central monolith of the circle is enclosed by its western edge. The tomb chamber is divided by upright slabs into two compartments. It has produced two fragments of bone, assumed to be human, but had clearly been robbed and partially dismantled in antiquity before the peat accumulated over it.

Among the many smaller stone settings around Callanish are several of unusual plan: an ellipse at Cnoc Ceann a'Gharaidh (Callanish II); a double-circle at Cnoc Fillibhir Bheag (Callanish III); and an impressive arc of stones overlooking the deep channel at Bernera Bridge (Callanish VIII). All are easily accessible.

3. Steinacleit (Lewis)

Accessible on foot, 500 m east of the A857 through Shader (NB 396541). In the care of Historic Scotland.

This is a complicated and superficially unimpressive site. The ruins of a structure of very large boulders – perhaps a chambered cairn – are overlain by a large oval foundation, probably that of a very large house or hall. The central mound is surrounded by a boulder wall, and at various points less substantial walls can be seen leading off under the peat, which covered the whole site until it was cut in the last century. These field walls may be of a different date both to the original cairn and to the subsequent house. The whole site may have been in use for various purposes from perhaps 3000 to 1500 BC.

Steincleit (Lewis).

The Iron Age: strong refuges (c.500 BC–AD c.560)

tudies of the past environment, based on the evidence of pollen preserved in boggy basins, suggest that after the natural scrub vegetation had been cleared from much of the Western Isles, a mixed farming economy was practised, with much open land under cultivation. As a result of climatic change, causing sightly cooler temperatures and wetter summers, and possibly hastened by over-grazing and poor farming techniques, a blanket of peat began to form on the higher ground, extending downhill gradually from around 1500 BC. This would have been accompanied by a reduction in the productivity of the land, the gradual abandonment and eventual burying of settlements on the upper slopes, and an increasing concentration of people on the coastal fringes.

By the end of the Bronze Age, perhaps around 500 BC, a major change affected society, as in the whole of Britain. This is reflected archaeologically in the appearance of new forms of settlement, designed for defence. Nowhere is this change more obvious than in the Western Isles, where the archaeological record, almost empty for the Bronze Age, is represented in the Iron Age by over a hundred fortified sites.

This change looks dramatic when viewed from the perspective of two millennia. But it may have been gradual, as groups of people, quite possibly drawn together by ties of kinship and threatened by land shortage and increasing strife with their neighbours, sought out more easily defended places and moved their homes there. Islands in lochs and cliff-girt promontories were probably the first natural choices – easy to fortify with a simple wall, and not too inconvenient for working the nearby fields or tending cattle. Perhaps these duns, as they are now called (from the Gaelic word for 'fort'), were originally used as temporary refuges, but

Dun an Sticir, Kildonan (S.Uist).

over time they became permanent. The loch islands were given stouter walls and stone buildings were erected within. Access, originally by small boats, was provided by boulder causeways, built to lie just below the surface and following a sinuous course to impede the approach of any unfamiliar visitor.

The technique of building fortifications was later elaborated, both for defence and also probably for prestige. The early simple designs were modified. Walls were heightened and the device of hollowing out the wall with an internal gallery allowed this to be achieved without placing too great an extra load on the foundations. In time there emerged the classic Iron Age monument of the Scottish north and west: the broch. Of these, Dun Carloway (Lewis)(see page 19) is one of the best-preserved examples.

The Western Isles have relatively few surviving identifiable brochs of the classic type with characteristic hollow drystone walling, superimposed galleries and linking stair, a single narrow entrance and a tall tapering profile. But many Iron Age fortifications are so ruined that it cannot be said whether they are duns or brochs. One interesting feature of the Western Isles' brochs is that they are generally sited in reasonably accessible

locations – as if the broch tower was felt to be defence enough without the added help of nature.

Brochs were essentially tall timber roundhouses encased in stone shells. For all the constructional skills displayed in building them, their inhabitants seem to have lived much the same sort of life as those around them, though some archaeological research has hinted that the diet of broch dwellers may have been rather better, with more meat and a wider range of crops and plants being consumed. This could support the view that brochs represented the high-status dwellings of the local leaders of Iron Age society, for whom the prestige of a high tower commanding the landscape probably counted as much as the security that it afforded.

Despite the considerable amount of research that has been undertaken on brochs, it has proved difficult to tie down a sequence of development, or to identify where the form first emerged. According to one view, they

Dun Cuier (Barra), broch.

were designed by specialist builders, who travelled around the Atlantic coast of Scotland, contracting out their skills to local communities. More fruitful has been the archaeological work undertaken on the lifestyle of the brochs' inhabitants at sites such as Dun Vulan (South Uist) and Loch na Berie (Lewis).

At some date as yet unknown, perhaps around AD 150, the perceived need for defence seems to have declined, at least for a time, and a new form of monumental roundhouse emerged, the so-called 'wheelhouse'. The name is inspired by the plan: a circular outer wall with radial internal sub-divisions. More so than the broch or the dun, the wheelhouse is a Western Isles speciality, few being known elsewhere except in Shetland.

Wheelhouses were elegant structures, using relatively little stone to provide a large internal space. They were tall and quite comfortable. A good idea of their appearance can be gained from the example excavated at Cnip, in Uig. Because wheelhouses were often built partly below ground on sandy sites, they have frequently become buried, and occasionally emerge as shorelines are eroded or as people dig into dunes for building sand.

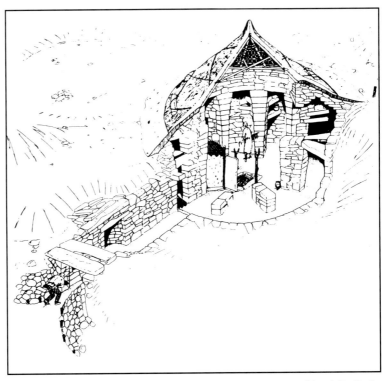

Cnip, Uig (Lewis): wheelhouse I, as reconstructed by A.R. Braby.

As well as forts, duns, brochs and wheelhouses, a range of other building forms are known from the Iron Age, but little is known about them. Simple oval huts have been found, as have circular house foundations, or hut circles. In some cases, these were built into earlier remains, notably chambered cairns, as at Clettraval (North Uist). One odd group of structures is represented by the souterrains, or earthhouses, subterranean passages built near or beneath houses, probably as storage places.

One problem for students of the Iron Age is that in material terms it did not end until fairly recently. Duns and even some brochs continued to be occupied into the Middle Ages, types of pottery changed little, and few exotic items which might assist archaeologists in dating sites seem to have been imported from other regions. The changes that the advent of Christianity brought about in the sixth and seventh centuries AD seem to have been intellectual and artistic, rather than social or economic.

Iron Age site to visit:

4. Dun Carloway, broch (Lewis)

Located in Doune Carloway township, signposted from the A858 (NB 191412). Accessible by foot, 100 m uphill from car park. In the care of Historic Scotland.

Dun Carloway is the best-preserved broch in the Western Isles, and one of the finest in Scotland. It still stands in part almost 9 m high, close to its original height. The collapse of part of its wall provides a cross-section showing the typical double-skinned wall with two tiers of internal galleries formed by flat slabs, which also serve to tie the wall together. As with all brochs, the plan is almost circular.

At ground level the wall is pierced by a narrow entrance, provided with checks for a wooden door-frame. A small cell in the thickness of the wall opens from the right-hand side of the entrance passage, perhaps to house a guard, or a dog. At this level the wall is part-solid, and part-hollow; but about 2m above ground level the continuous galleries begin. On the inside face of the wall at the level of the lower gallery is a stone ledge or scarcement, which may have supported either a raised floor or the edge of a roof. The main weight of this floor or roof, however, would have been carried by a ring of timber posts.

Long after the wooden structures had been removed or rotted, the shell and chambers of the broch were used as a storage place and occasional habitation. Interestingly, the ruin was not plundered for building stone, a fact which suggests that the broch, even as a ruin, was still regarded as a place of importance.

Dun Carloway (Lewis), broch.

The foundation of the monastery of Iona by St Columba in AD 563 was a key event in the process by which the Christian message was spread from Ireland to western Scotland during the later sixth and seventh centuries. Unfortunately the historical sources that record the evangelisation of the Iron Age Scots and Picts say little of the Western Isles. St Columba himself came no nearer than Skye, and it is therefore uncertain whether it was from Iona or from some other missionary source that Christianity was introduced into these islands.

That Christianity arrived at an early date, however, is suggested by the evidence of archaeology and place-names. Near the ruined late medieval church at Bagh Bàn, on the east side of Pabbay (Barra), a rough slab of stone has been found bearing incised on it two Pictish symbols (the lily and the crescent and V-rod) beneath a Latin cross. Three other cross-incised slabs, originally used as grave-markers, also come from this site; and others have been discovered on Berneray (Barra) and Hirta (St Kilda)*(see left)*. A pair of stone crosses, which stand in Cill Mhoire kirkyard, Hougharry (North Uist), were probably erected in the mid-eighth century; they have stumpy arms and circles cut in the four re-entrant angles, while one also has a raised boss at the intersection of the vertical and horizontal members.

The place-name Pabbay, or Papay, which occurs eight times in the Western Isles and is derived from the Norse *papar-øy*, meaning 'priests' island', may also indicate the existence of Christian clergy before the Viking settlement. But while numerous church dedications still survive to Irish saints, including Columba, Bride (or Brigit), Maclrubha, Ronan and Moluag, it is possible that many of these are post-Norse in origin.

In its organisation the Celtic church was monastic, with a network of communities of monks or individual hermits' cells dependent on a mother church, such as Iona. In the Western Isles, remains of churches securely datable before the

(top left) Hirta (St Kilda): Early Christian cross-incised stone.
(right) Bagh Bàn, Pabbay (Barra): Pictish symbol stone and cross.

Viking raids are rare, though it is likely that many lie beneath later medieval chapels and graveyards. Some 400 m south-east of Balivanich (Benbecula), for example, the remains of a later medieval church of St Columba (Teampall Chaluim Chille) occupy a slight knoll in the midst of a marsh; to the west of this, another similar knoll, on which there are traces of buildings, may possibly represent the monastic enclosure attached to the church.

The best-preserved buildings of this date, however, lie in remote places and owe their survival to the fact that they were not rebuilt or replaced in later times. On Eilean Mór, the larger of the Flannan Isles, stand the remains of a small stone-built chapel of Irish type, which probably once formed part of a hermitage. A low narrow door with inward sloping sides, set in the west gable wall, leads into an interior space, roofed by corbelling the side walls inwards. Remains of another possible hermitage survive on Luchruban, or the Pigmies' Isle, a stack of rock rising from the sea 1.6km west-south-west of the Butt of Lewis. These consist of a rectangular and a rounded corbelled structure, possibly a chapel and living cell respectively, surrounded by an oval stone enclosure wall.

Early Christian site to visit:

5. St Ronan's Chapel, Rona (Ronaidh)

Located on the island of Rona, 72 km (44 miles) NNE of the Butt of Lewis, accessible by boat from Ness only in calm weather (HW 809323). A National Nature Reserve in the care of Scottish Natural Heritage, from whom permission to land should be sought.

The island of Rona (or North Rona, as it is sometimes called) is triangular in shape and about 15 ha in area, rising to a maximum altitude of 108 m. Its last inhabitant left in 1844, and, except for seasonal visits by shepherds and naturalists, it is now deserted. Its principal monuments include the chapel of St Ronan, standing within an oval cemetery enclosure, three groups of sunken corbelled dwellings, apparently of medieval origin though occupied in part well into the nineteenth century, and a well-preserved open field system comprising narrow rigs enclosed by a head-dyke.

Although St Ronan is a historical figure, mentioned by his early eighth-century contemporary, the

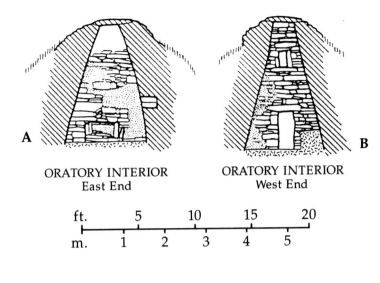

A ORATORY INTERIOR
East End

B ORATORY INTERIOR
West End

ft. 5 10 15 20
m. 1 2 3 4 5

*(Top) Chapel, cemetery and field system
from SW*

*(Bottom) Entrance to the 'oratory', showing
grave markers from cemetery*

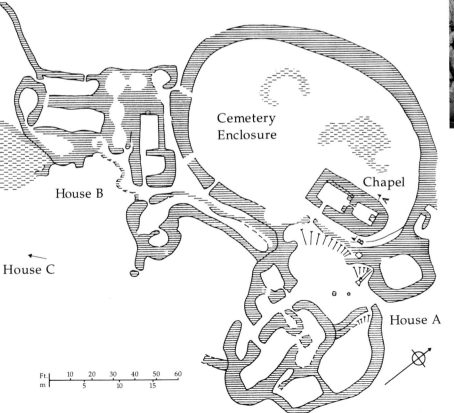

Cemetery
Enclosure

Chapel

House B

House C

House A

Ft. 10 20 30 40 50 60
m. 5 10 15

Venerable Bede, his association with Rona is attested only by later oral tradition. According to legend, Ronan came to Rona from Eoropie (Lewis) on the back of a whale, to escape the noise of scolding and quarrelsome women; having battled successfully against the Devil, who assailed him with a storm and a pack of monstrous dog-like creatures and serpents, he built the small corbelled chapel that still stands there today. That the chapel with its enclosure was originally built in the late seventh or early eighth century as a hermitage, dependent on a mainland church such as Eoropie, seems very likely. But the name Rona probably comes from the Norse, *hraun-øy*, meaning 'rough island', and may therefore originally have had nothing to do with St Ronan at all.

The chapel has two parts: an eastern chamber known as 'the oratory' or 'St Ronan's cell', measuring some 3.4 by 2.1 m internally and enclosed by a corbelled roof 3.2 m high; and to the west of this a larger outer cell, some 4.6 by 3.3 m internally, now unroofed but probably once covered by a roof of driftwood, turf and straw thatch. The eastern chamber was evidently the original chapel. It is entered through a low narrow door in the west gable. The wall is slightly concave on the outside, the result – according to tradition – of the Devil's attempts to blow it down. Inside, against its east wall stands the base of a stone altar, and in the south wall next to it is a small niche where the communion vessels would have been kept. The outer chamber may possibly have been added later, to accommodate more people as the community expanded. Certainly, in the later seventeenth century this was the part used as a chapel by the island's inhabitants, though there was at that time no priest. It is equally possible, however, that the original function of the outer chamber was as the living cell of the founder of the hermitage.

The chapel lies in the south-eastern part of an oval enclosure, extending for some 32 by 19 m and surrounded by an earth and stone bank. Within this, north-west of the chapel, the remains of a stone cist, possibly for a grave or shrine, have been noted. The collection of cross-marked grave slabs from the cemetery includes types indicative of the two early periods of occupation of the site: the first from the seventh century to the ninth, and the second from the twelfth century to the thirteenth. One of the finest examples from the latter group is now on display in Ness Heritage Centre (Lewis).

It seems likely that the hermitage would have been abandoned when Viking raids began to affect the Western Isles around the year 800. When Rona was resettled in the twelfth or thirteenth century, its new inhabitants appear to have been secular. Probably, as in later times, they came from Ness, and made their precarious living from agriculture, and from harvesting the plentiful supply of fish and wildfowl. It may also have been they who built the three groups of domestic buildings, two adjoining the south-west side of the enclosure and another lying a little way to the west. These belong to a general type of structure that was probably common throughout the Western Isles from the late Iron Age, and persisted in some areas until the mid-nineteenth century. The buildings are constructed partly below ground. Each group contains a long narrow subrectangular living room, originally roofed in timber and straw thatch, surrounded by a series of smaller oval rooms, corbelled in stone. These structures partly enclose an open oval courtyard, from which a byre and granary are also accessible. Each building complex seems to have been intended to accommodate a family, together with its livestock and grain supply.

The hermitage on Rona is one of the most complete groups of buildings of the early Celtic Church to survive anywhere in Scotland. Unfortunately the extreme difficulty of gaining access means that even today it is visited by only the most intrepid.

Rona, St Ronan's chapel, from N.

The Norse settlement (c.800–1266)

Viking raids began to affect the north-west coasts of Scotland in the last decade of the eighth century. In 795 Iona was devastated, and in 798 the Annals of Ulster record that the Hebrides and north of Ireland were plundered. These early hit-and-run raids, however, were followed around 840 by a phase of settlement.

The Western Isles were evidently intensively settled by the Norse, to the extent that the islands themselves came to be known to mainland Celts as *Innse Gall*, or the 'Islands of the Foreigners'. While archaeology has so far been able to tell us little about the process and nature of the settlement, place-names constitute a more informative source of evidence. It has been estimated, for instance, that of the 126 village names in Lewis, 99 are purely Scandinavian in origin and a further nine contain Norse elements. Some of the commonest forms are those containing the elements *-bólstadr* (homestead), *-stadir* (farm, or dwelling place) and *-setr* (dwelling-place or summer pasture). Examples include Siabost, Mealabost, Garrabost, Tolastadh, Mealasta, Griomsiadar, Linsiader. Norse elements also predominate in the names of natural features lying close to or visible from the sea. These include elements such as *-ay* or *-øy* (island), *-fjall* (hill) and *-nes* (headland), which occur, albeit in gaelicised form, in Scalpaigh, Bearnaraigh, Tarasaigh, Roineabhal, Griomaval, Heaval, Griminis, Horsanis and Stocinis. Towards the southern end of the island chain the proportion of Norse to Gaelic settlement names decreases; but it is not certain whether this should be taken to indicate that Norse settlement was more thinly spread, or that the gaelicisation of place-names at a later date was simply more thorough than elsewhere.

The Scandinavian settlers of the ninth and tenth centuries were pagans, worshipping the Norse gods, Thor, Odin and others. Their graves may be distinguished from those of the Christians amongst whom they settled by the inclusion in them of objects of daily use, intended to accompany the deceased on the journey to the afterlife. In some areas, these goods might include the owner's boat, horse, and sometimes even a wife or slave. In the Western Isles, such graves as have been discovered appear to have been quite modestly provisioned. A grave at Valtos (Lewis), for example, contained a pair of large 'tortoise' brooches along with other personal ornaments of Celtic type. Similar pairs of brooches have also been found on St Kilda; and on Barra two separate graves contained a broadly similar range of goods, including in each case a pair of 'tortoise' brooches, a sword, a shield, a whetstone, buckles and a comb.

In 995, Olaf Tryggvasson, king of Norway, forced Sigurd, earl of Orkney, to abandon paganism and accept Christianity. Indeed, it appears to have been political pressure from above, rather than evangelisation at local level, that proved decisive in bringing about the conversion of the Norse settlers of Britain and Ireland in the early eleventh century. Christian influence of a Scandinavian type (hence Roman as opposed to Celtic) may be detected in church dedications such as those to St Aulay (Olaf) at Gress (Lewis), and, though at a much later date, to St Clement at Rodel (Harris).

By the end of the eleventh century, all the western islands of Scotland, which the Norwegians knew as the *Sudreyar*, or 'Southern Isles', to distinguish them from the *Nordreyar*, or 'Northern Isles' (Orkney and Shetland), formed part of the Norse kingdom of Man and the Isles; this was in turn dependent on the king of Norway. In 1156, Somerled mac Gille-Brigde, a Celto-Norse ruler of Lorn (Argyll), revolted against the king of Man, and succeeded in wresting from him control of the *Sudreyar* lying south of Ardnamurchan Point. Somerled's death at the hands of Malcolm IV's troops near Renfrew in 1164,

and the subsequent splitting of his inheritance, provided the Scottish king with the opportunity for extending his own authority into the island regions of Argyll and the Clyde estuary. For the time being, the islands lying north of Ardnamurchan, including the Western Isles and Skye, remained subject to

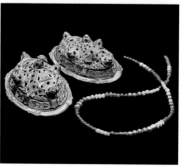

(top left) The Kingdom of Man, c.1150. Seal of Harald, King of Man and the Isles, 1246.
(right) Tortoise brooches and other objects from a Viking grave at Valtos.
(top right) Part of a collection of 78 chess pieces of 12th-century date, known as the 'Lewis chessmen' found by a crofter in Uig (Lewis) in 1831.

Norway. In 1263, however, King Haakon IV made a final attempt to retake and hold Bute and Kintyre; as his fleet made its way south, it drew support from the Celto-Norse inhabitants of the Western Isles and Islay. But following an inconclusive skirmish with the Scots at Largs, the king withdrew, to die in Kirkwall (Orkney) on his return journey to Bergen. Three years later, by the treaty of Perth, the entire kingdom of Man and the Isles was ceded to Alexander III by Haakon's successor, Magnus. For the Western Isles, this marked the effective end to the period of Norse domination.

Norse-period site to visit:

6. Cille Bharra (Barra), St Barr's Chapel and rune-inscribed cross

Located in a cemetery, 1 km N of the airport, and easily accessible by road or foot (NF 704074). In the care of the Roman Catholic Church.

The principal saint of the island of Barra, from whom it derives its name, *Barr-øy*, meaning 'Barr's Island' in Norse, was St Barr, or Finnbarr. Although tradition equates him with the sixth-century Irish saint, Finbar of Cork, a later medieval Life preserved in the Aberdeen Breviary records that he was a Gaelic Scot, born the illegitimate son of a Caithness nobleman and ordained priest by Pope Gregory the Great. His feast day is still celebrated on 27 September. The church of St Barr at Cille Bharra was therefore quite possibly a pre-Norse foundation, established as early as the

seventh century; from it may have depended the hermitage at Bagh Bàn on Pabbay (see page 21).

Norse sagas relate that the first Viking to come to Barra was Onund Wooden-Leg, who arrived with five ships in 871 and drove out the local king, Kiarval. Subsequently he used Barra as winter quarters for his raiding expeditions further south.

Place-names suggest that Norse settlement in Barra was less intensive than that further north in Lewis. Graphic archaeological evidence for the mingling of

Cille Bharra (Barra), from S.

Celtic and Norse culture in the island, however, is provided by the rare discovery of a rune stone in the cemetery of Cille Bharra in 1865. The original is now in the Royal Museum of Scotland in Edinburgh, but a cast is displayed in the roofed chapel in the cemetery.

The stone is an irregular slab, some 1.37 m high. The runic inscription covers one face and may be transcribed and translated as follows:

> [...]TIR THUR KIRTHU S[...] IN [...] R
> [...]R IS KURS SIA RISTA
> [...]A

> *After Thorgerth, Steiner's daughter,*
> *this cross was raised.*

Cille Bharra (Barra), rune stone and cross.

On the other face the stone is carved with a cross of Celtic type, decorated with thickly plaited interlace. The style of the decoration suggests a date in the late tenth or eleventh century; it may be compared with the large group of cross-slabs on the Isle of Man, where Celtic and Norse art forms experienced a similar cross-fertilisation.

St Barr's church seems to have contin-

Cille Bharra (Barra), plan of church and chapels.

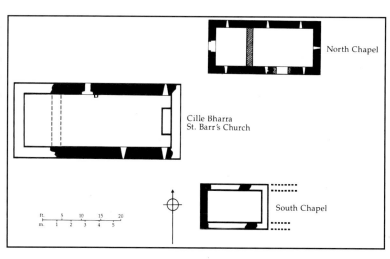

North Chapel

Cille Bharra
St. Barr's Church

South Chapel

ft.   5   10   15   20
m.   1   2   3   4   5

ued as a parish church throughout the Middle Ages. In fact, the cemetery contains today the remains of three ruined buildings, none of which seems likely to be earlier than twelfth century. The largest, evidently the parish church, lies to the west of the other two, which appear to have been dependent chapels. It had a plain rectangular plan, measuring overall 13.1 by 5.6 m. Though the gables have fallen, the door in the north wall can be seen to have the inward-sloping jambs that

are typical of early medieval Irish church architecture; the heads of the narrow splayed windows are rounded externally and triangular on the inside. The base of a stone altar survives against the east wall. The only medieval mention of this church is in 1402, when the anti-pope, Benedict XIII, confirmed Gelisius Martini (Gill-Iosa mac Gille-Martin) to the vicarage, which had previously been held by Martin de Servgrant.

Little remains of the south chapel. The north chapel, however, has been re-roofed to house the cast of the rune stone and three later medieval tombstones. These date to the early sixteenth century, and probably once covered the graves of Macneill chiefs of Barra or their relatives. Two show a sword set in a design of floral interlace; the other has a galley with furled sail surrounded by interlace, with a stag at the base.

Cille Bharra (Barra), early 16th-century gravestone, probably of one of the Macneills.

Of the former Norwegian possessions that had been ceded to him in 1266 by the Treaty of Perth, King Alexander III granted Lewis, Harris and Skye to Ferquhard Macintagart, earl of Ross. The remainder of the Western Isles he bestowed on the Clann MhicRuairidh, the former Norse holders of Bute. But although the Western Isles were now legally subject to the Scottish king, during the fourteenth century most of them and the Inner Hebrides were brought together as a single lordship, the lordship of the Isles. This was to remain virtually independent of royal authority until the end of the fifteenth century.

In 1337 John Macdonald of Islay, who was then holding Lewis, married Amy, the sister of Raghnall MhicRuaridh, lord of Uist, Benbecula and Barra. When Raghnall was murdered in 1346, leaving no son, his possessions passed to her, and thereby to John of Islay. In 1350, however, John put Amy aside in order to marry Margaret, the eldest daughter of Robert Stewart, later to become King Robert II (1371–90). From 1354, with all the Outer and Inner Hebrides except Skye under his control, John of Islay began styling himself 'lord of the Isles' (*dominus insularum*).

The lord of the Isles controlled much of the lordship indirectly, by granting parts of it to his kinsmen. In 1373 John, first lord of the Isles, granted the former MhicRuaridh inheritance, including Eigg, Rum, Uist, Barra and St Kilda, to Reginald (Ranald), his son by his first wife, from whom the Clan Ranald takes its name. North Uist passed to Godfrey, Ranald's brother. By the end of the fourteenth century Lewis was being held by the descendants of Torquil MacLeod (the Siol Thorcuil). And in 1427 Alexander, third lord of the Isles, granted Barra and much of South Uist to Gill-Adhamnain Macneill.

The period of the lordship of the Isles may justly be regarded as the golden age of medieval culture and society in the Isles. While they remained technically part of the Scottish kingdom, the feudal system of land-holding and personal obligation imposed from above mingled at a lower level with the traditional structures of Gaelic society based on ties of kinship. Justice was administered through the Council of the Isles, consisting of the principal island chiefs meeting with the lord at one of his castles, such as Tingwall, or on the Council Isle in Finlaggan Loch, Islay. Although warfare was extolled as a heroic virtue by the Macdonald poets of the age and tombstones of the late fourteenth and fifteenth centuries show island leaders armoured and clasping broadswords, the lord of the Isles generally contrived to maintain peace within his realm. If the islanders appeared warlike to outsiders, this was because warfare became an article of export, both through the activities of mercenaries and through the vigorous means by which the lordship maintained its independence from mainland interference.

The lordship of the Isles came to an end in 1493, when John, fourth lord, was forfeited; his lands were subsequently annexed by the crown. The pattern of land-holding in the Isles, however, continued largely as before, with a small number of important families predominating. In the south, the Macneills enjoyed full possession of Barra and South Uist until 1621, thereafter continuing as tenants of Sir Roderick Mackenzie of Kintail. In 1495 James IV confirmed Hugh Macdonald of Sleat (in Skye) in possession of North Uist, Benbecula and the northern part of South Uist, which had been granted him by John, fourth lord of the Isles in 1469. In 1498 Alexander MacLeod of Dunvegan was likewise confirmed in possession of Western Skye and Harris (including St Kilda). Lewis remained in the hands of the Macleods of Lewis until 1610, when James VI granted it to Kenneth Mackenzie of Kintail, from whom were descended the earls of Seaforth.

The support given by successive earls of Seaforth to the Stewarts resulted in the occupation of Stornoway by Cromwell's troops in 1653, and in the fifth earl forfeiting his estates following the abortive Jacobite risings of 1715 and 1719. They were restored in 1741 to the sixth earl, who, unlike his southerly Roman Catholic neighbours, the Macdonalds and Macneills, remained loyal to the Government during the rebellion of 1745.

efore the eighteenth century, historical sources tell us more about the lifestyle of the higher levels of island society than about the inhabitants of villages and shielings, whose labours made that lifestyle possible. Unfortunately, upstanding archaeological remains, by their nature, tend to reinforce rather counterpoise this imbalance in the evidence. For what we know of domestic architecture of this period relates almost exclusively to the more solidly built residences of clan leaders and their extended families, rather than to the humbler dwellings of the vast majority of the population.

As in Ireland and other parts of the Celtic west, a number of forts (duns and crannogs) that had served as the principal residences of local chiefs in late Iron Age times continued to be occupied as such throughout the Middle Ages. Indeed, some dun-like structures appear to be medieval in origin. The best examples are in the Uists, where the low-lying, partly submerged landscape favoured the development of island duns as places of security. Dun Aonais (or Aonghais), for example, situated in Loch Aonghais (North Uist), takes its name from Aonghas Fionn (Angus the Fair), who is supposed to have lived in it in the sixteenth century. Dun Ban, in Loch Caravat (North Uist), consists of a D-shaped enclosure wall built in lime-mortared rubble masonry. The outer gate, recessed in the curve of the D, led into an open court, beyond which a rectangular hall (15.7 by 5.9m internally) occupied the straight side of the enclosure.

Some other island refuges display more obvious signs of medieval fortification. Dun Mhic Leoid (or Castle Sinclair), for example, situated on an islet in Loch Tangusdale (Barra), includes a masonry tower, originally three storeys high and measuring 2.9 by 2.6 m internally within walls 1.4 m thick. Another tower, known as Caisteal Bheagram, situated at the centre of a circular island enclosed by a wall in Loch an Eilein,

(top) Castle represented on the tomb of Alexander MacLeod (1528) in St Clement's Church, Rodel (Harris).
(left) Dun Ban (N. Uist), reconstruction drawing.

(top) Dun Mhic Leoid (Barra).
(above) Caisteal Bheagram (S. Uist).

near Howmore (South Uist), is not much larger, measuring 3.1 by 3.9m internally, with walls 1.1-1.4 m thick. The owner of this castle, Ranald Alansoun of Ylandbigrim, was evidently of some means, for in 1505 he was confirmed in possession of the castle of Dun Sgathaich and certain lands in Sleat parish, Skye. The small size of both these towers, however, suggests that they were intended less as residences than as refuges, vantage points and status symbols; for the remains of more traditionally constructed domestic buildings lie near by.

The Western Isles have very few major stone-built castles of the kind that were constructed in such numbers in Argyll and the Inner Hebrides from the later thirteenth century onwards. This may have been due in part to the fact that feudalism, of which castles were an overt material expression, was less firmly rooted here than in those areas brought more closely under Scottish royal control. It may also have been the result of a social structure in which power was concentrated in the hands of a very few major families.

Castle Calvay, occupying a rocky islet at the mouth of Loch Boisdale (South Uist), is the closest thing to a castle of enclosure to be found in the Western Isles. The enclosure is irregular, covering the summit of the island, and against its inner face are the remains of collapsed buildings. On the north side, a two-storey building, measuring some 10.5 by 5 m overall, evidently represents the hall block, while in the south-west corner are the foundations of a small tower. Nothing is known of this castle's history. Stornoway Castle, whose remains now lie beneath the ferry pier, was the stronghold of the Macleods of Lewis from early in the sixteenth century. What little we know of it, before its destruction by Cromwell's troops in 1653, suggests that it consisted of a tower-house and an outer wall enclosing a hall and other buildings.

Remains of another tower or hall-house, known as Borve Castle, stand just north-west of Lionacleit (Benbecula). This can probably be identified with the castle of *Vynvawle* in the island of Uist (*insula de Huwyste*), that is mentioned in a royal charter of 1372/3 as forming part of the lands granted to Ranald, son of John of Islay, and with *Benwevil*, that is included in John of Fordun's list of castles of the same period. A later owner, Ranald of Castellborf, is mentioned in 1625. The remains are of a rectangular structure with very thick walls, measuring some 15 by 12 m overall; but the building is now too badly ruined to allow one to tell exactly when it was built.

This chronological sequence of castles concludes with Ormacleit Castle (South Uist), built in 1701 as the residence of Ailean, chief of Clan Ranald; it was burnt out in 1715 and never rebuilt. The building is unfortified and consists of a two-storey house, T-shaped in plan, facing north on to a courtyard, which is enclosed on the west by an earlier range containing a spacious kitchen fireplace. Over the doorway can be seen an armorial panel, similar to one that formerly existed at Howmore (see page 42).

(left) Borve Castle (Benbecula).
(below) Ormacleit Castle (S.Uist)

Medieval castle to visit:

7. Kisimul Castle (Barra)

Kisimul Castle (Barra), from S.

Located on a rock in Castlebay harbour and accessible only by boat from the shore (NL 665979). In the private ownership of Macneil of Barra, and open by appointment.

In 1549 Dean Monro described Kisimul as 'ane castell in ane Ile upon ane strenthie craig callit Keselum perteining to Mcneill of Barray'. The Macneills were the descendants of Gill-Adhamnain Macneill, who had received possession of Barra by a charter of Alexander Macdonald, lord of the Isles, on 23 June 1427. Although it is very possible that the rock on which it stands had already been fortified in earlier times, there is nothing about the existing medieval structure to suggest a date earlier than the middle of the fifteenth century.

That the castle could put up a stiff defence was shown in 1675, when some crown officials attempting to serve a writ on the owner were met by 'foure scoir shott of hagbutts, guns and pistolls', and by large stones hurled from the walls. In 1695, Kisimul was seen by Martin Martin, who records: 'There is a stone Wall round it two stories high, reaching the Sea, and within the Wall there is an old Tower and an Hall, with other Houses about it. There is a little Magazine in the Tower, to which no Stranger has access. I saw the Officer call'd the *Cockman* [i.e. watchman], and an old Cock he is: when I bid him ferry me over the Water to the Island, he told me that he was but an inferior Officer ... but if (says he) the Constable, who then stood on the Wall, will give you access, I'll ferry you over.' After waiting some hours for an answer, Martin gave up his attempted visit. The owner at this time, whose absence was the cause of difficulty, was Ruari Dhu Macneill, an inveterate raider and passionate Jacobite, who had fought for John Graham, Viscount Dundee, at Killiecrankie in 1689 and would follow James Stewart in 1715. The constable may therefore have had good cause to feel apprehensive.

By the mid-eighteenth century the castle had been abandoned, and in 1795 its roofs and floors were burnt. It lay in ruins until 1937, when the chief of Clan Macneil, the Canadian Robert Lister Macneil, acquired the estate of Barra. The site was cleared of rubble, and between 1956 and Robert Lister's death in 1970, the castle was restored and made habitable once more.

The castle's form is similar to that of other West Highland castles of the period, such as Breachacha (Coll) and Dunollie (Argyll), with a rectangular tower-house set to one side of an irregular enclosure containing other buildings. In Kisimul's case, the roughly pentagonal shape of the enclosure was determined by that of the island. The original entrance, with portcullis, was on the east; but it was moved closer to the tower when the watchman's house was enlarged in the sixteenth century. Just outside the gate lie the remains of the building that housed the crew of the lord's galley.

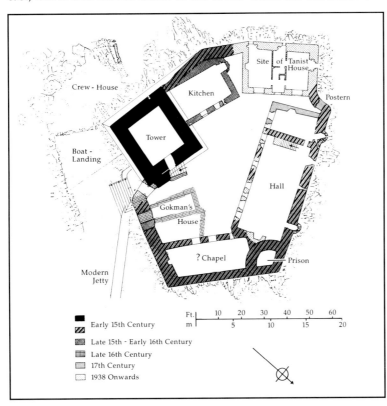

The tower, standing at the south-east corner, was evidently the first element of the castle to be built. It rises three-storeys high. The basement, probably used for storage, was entered through a door in the north wall, reached up a stair; internal access would only have been possible through a trap in the first floor. The external staircase continued in timber up to the adjacent curtain wall walk, from which another timber stair, cantilevered from the face of the tower, gave access to the main door, 5.5 m above ground level. Inside, a stair within the thickness of the wall led up to the second floor and down to the first. All the floors were of timber, as was the roof.

The first and second floors were evidently domestic in purpose, both being well lit and having latrine closets within their walls. Both also had timber galleries or sleeping lofts at their north ends, that above the second floor being in effect within the garret. From the second floor, another mural stair leads from the right-hand side of the north window up to the wall-head. The crenellated parapet encloses a latrine in the south-west corner, and shows signs of later heightening on all but the north side. This later work, possibly of around 1500, included a box-machicolation projecting directly above the tower's entrance and allowing the defenders to drop missiles on the heads of unwelcome visitors; on the south and east, a timber wall-walk was carried on beams which ran through the parapet to support projecting external timber hoarding, designed to protect the tower's exposed outer faces in the same way.

The curtain wall abuts the tower and was evidently built later, though possibly not by much. Its parapet, like that of the tower, was also subsequently heightened and provided with a timber wall-walk (possibly also with projecting hoarding) and with a box-machicolation above the outer gate. The obtuse north angle was occupied by a rounded internal tower, standing apparently no higher than the wall and containing a pit-prison with latrine below a guard room. Against the north-west wall stood the hall; this was extended south-west and provided with an upper storey in the seventeenth century, when it quite possibly replaced the tower as the principal residence; it was restored in 1958–60. To the west of it is a postern gate. Another fifteenth-century building, now rebuilt as a chapel, occupied the north-east wall.

The other buildings constructed against the inside face of the curtain wall are of a later period. They include, on the south, a sixteenth-century kitchen range of two storeys adjoining the tower; in the west corner, the Tanist (or heir's) house, rebuilt in 1956–7 from its sixteenth-century foundations (and not accessible to visitors); and on the east, beside the entrance gate, the unrestored foundations of the sixteenth-century house of the Gokman (or watchman), whose seventeenth-century successor so taxed Martin's patience in 1695.

During the Norse period, the Western Isles, together with the Isle of Man and all the Scottish islands then under Norwegian control (with the exception of Orkney and Shetland), formed part of the diocese of Man and the Isles. This was subject to the archdiocese of York until 1153, and thereafter to Nidaros (or Trondheim) in Norway. By the treaty of Perth, in 1266, secular patronage of the see was transferred to the king of Scotland, but the archbishop of Trondheim retained spiritual superiority.

The early bishops of this straggling diocese were peripatetic, moving their episcopal seat, or *cathedra*, from place to place. By 1231, a cathedral and chapter had been established at Peel, in the Isle of Man; but in 1330 this was effectively cut off from the Scottish part of the diocese, when Man was seized by the English. In 1331 the canons of Snizort and the clergy of Skye, who had elected their own bishop, attempted to have him confirmed as such by the archbishop in Trondheim. The outcome is unknown; but from 1387 the see was formally split, with the bishop of Sodor and Man becoming subject (as today) to the archbishop of York, and a separate bishop of Sodor, or the Isles, being appointed to the Scottish part of the former diocese. The latter was placed under the authority of the archbishop of St Andrews in 1472, and by 1617 was subject to the archbishop of Glasgow.

The church on Skeabost Island, in the River Snizort, seems to have served as cathedral at least until 1433. In April 1498 a request was made to the pope to erect the Benedictine abbey on Iona into a cathedral. But although the bishop gained possession of the abbey's lands and revenues, there is no evidence that the monks ever consituted a cathedral chapter. None the less, a chapter on Iona is mentioned in 1547–8, and a dean and chapter of Sodor participated in the election of a new bishop in 1572/3. When cathedral chapters were restored in 1617, the abandoned abbey church on Iona did at last become cathedral for a short period, until the abolition of episcopacy in 1638.

From 1565 the bishops of the Isles were Protestants. In 1609 a synod consisting mostly of island chiefs, convened by Bishop Andrew Knox on Iona, issued a set of statutes, supporting the spread of the reformed religion through the islands and the repair of ruined churches. Whether the island populations chose to follow the old or new religion, however, often depended on the example set by their leaders. Thus, in the early seventeenth century the Macneills of Barra were Protestants and in 1609 the church of St Barr had a Protestant minister; but the arrival of Franciscan missionaries from Ireland in 1625 resulted in the conversion of the chief, and thereby most of the island, to Catholicism seven years later. Irish missionary activity continued into the eighteenth century, and this and clan loyalty largely accounts for the religious divide which still exists in the islands today, with a concentration of Catholics in the south and of Protestants in the north.

As organised religion assumed more importance in the lives of islanders of both communities, pre-Reformation church buildings came to be abandoned, less for sectarian reasons than because they were simply too small. The ruins of many of these structures still survive throughout the islands, though their graveyards are often still in use. Their characteristic form, whether they be early or late medieval in date, is of a small rectangular structure with a pitched roof, a door towards the west end of the south wall (or less often in the north or west wall), slit windows, the stone base for an altar against the east wall, and often a recess in the wall to the south of it where the vessels used in the Mass were kept. Good examples of this type of church building can be seen at Nunton

(Benbecula), Ensay (Harris), and Rudh' an Teampall, south-west of Northton (Harris).

Certain churches depart from the standard form. Teampall Eoin (St John's), at Bragar (Lewis), for example, has a projecting rectangular chancel separated from the nave by an arch; its date may perhaps be fifteenth century. It was only in the sixteenth century, however, that larger, more complex structures such as Teampall Mholuaidh, Eoropie (Lewis) (see page 47), and St Clement's, Rodel (Harris)(see page 49), came to be built.

Nunton Church (Benbecula).

Medieval churches to visit:

8. Tobha Mòr, Howmore (South Uist)

North of Howmore village, a walk of 100 m east past the youth hostel from the Church of Scotland parish church (NF 758365).

The ecclesiastical site at Howmore occupies what would at one time have been virtually an island, surrounded by marshes. It comprises the remains of two churches and of two chapels, a third chapel (Caibeal na Sagairt) having been demolished by 1866. Although the grouping of individual churches and chapels on one site and certain of their architectural features, such as steeply pitched gables and inward sloping doorways, are reminiscent of early Irish church practice, none of the existing structures at Howmore seems likely to date earlier than the thirteenth century. The parish of Howmore is first mentioned in the fourteenth century, and in the sixteenth it constituted a parsonage dependent on the abbey of Iona.

By the end of the sixteenth century, and quite possibly earlier, the site was noted as the burial place of the chiefs of Clan Ranald, who had held South Uist since the 1370s. The first such burial to be recorded by the *Book of Clan Ranald*, a compilation of the seventeenth century, was that of Eoin Muideartach, who left funds to build a chapel at Howmore, where he was buried in 1574.

The first building to be reached as one approaches the site from the

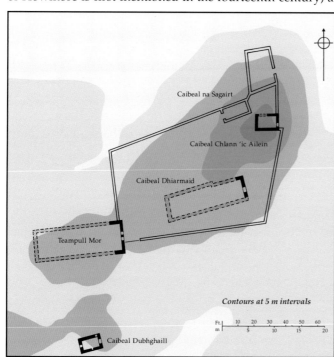

Howmore (S. Uist): plan of the site (based on survey by University of Sheffield).

Caibeal na Sagairt

Caibeal Chlann 'ic Ailein

Caibeal Dhiarmaid

Teampull Mor

Contours at 5 m intervals

Caibeal Dubhghaill

west is Teampall Mór (St Mary's, or the Large Church). By Western Isles standards, this was indeed a large church, measuring some 20 by 8 m and built, like the other buildings at Howmore, in rubble masonry set in a white lime mortar. Only the east gable is now standing; it contains two narrow splayed windows with segmental heads and semi-circular rear-arches, below and to either side of which are a pair of rectangular aumbries (or wall-cupboards). This was evidently the parish church, and, although there is little evidence to go on, a thirteenth-century date seems quite possible.

To the south of this lies Caibeal Dubhghaill, or Chlann 'ic Dhubhghaill (Dugall's Chapel, or the Chapel of the Kindred of the Son of Dugall). This is a small structure, measuring only 5.2 by 3.5 m, with high-pitched gables and a door on the east with inward sloping sides. A small slit-window is set above the door and in each of the other three walls.

Caibeal Dhiarmaid (St Dermot's Chapel), also known in 1695 as St Columba's, lies 30 m east of Teampall Mór. It was evidently slightly smaller, being 5.7 m wide, but of unknown length. A single window pierces the remaining east gable wall. Below and to the left of it a projecting corbel possibly once supported the altar table, while to the right there is a wall-cupboard. In the grass-covered nave, a cross-marked stone slab, possibly of Early Christian date, has been used to mark a later grave.

The fourth building, Caibeal Chlann 'ic Ailein (Clan Ranald's Chapel), lies at the north-east corner of the graveyard. It may be assumed that this was the chapel constructed with Eoin Muideartach's bequest in 1574. The door, now blocked, was formerly in the east gable. Until 1990, when it was mysteriously removed, an armorial panel of Clan Ranald could be seen lying inside it. The chapel also contains a piece of stone decorated in dog-tooth, probably of thirteenth-century date; this may have come from either of the two churches at Howmore.

(top) Howmore (S.Uist): Teampall Mór, with Caibeal Dhiarmaid behind.
(left) Howmore (S. Uist): Caibeal Chlann 'ic Ailean (Clan Ranald's Chapel) (1574).

9. Teampall na Trionaid (Church of the Holy Trinity), Carinish (North Uist)

200 m walk north-west across farm land from parking place beside the road (NF 816603).
In private ownership.

The seventeenth-century *Book of Clan Ranald* attributes the foundation of Teampall na Trionaid to Bethag, daughter of Somerled and first prioress of the Augustinian nunnery on Iona. Other oral traditions hold it to have been an important place of learning in the early Middle Ages, at which the Franciscan philosopher Duns Scotus (*c.*1265–1309), among others, received part of his education. Whatever the truth of such traditions, a 'chapel of the Holy Trinity in Uist' certainly existed by the early fourteenth century, when it was granted along with 'the whole land of Carinish and four pennylands in Illeray' to the abbey of Inchaffray in Perthshire by Christina MhicRuairidh, the aunt of Amy, first wife of John of Islay. This grant was confirmed in 1389 by Amy's son Godfrey, lord of North Uist, and again in 1410 by his brother Donald, lord of the Isles. By *c.*1561, however, Carinish was listed among the lands of the abbot of Iona, and in 1575 it was being held from the bishop by James Macdonald of Castle Camus.

The church features in accounts of the battle of Carinish between the Macdonalds and a raiding party of MacLeods from Harris, in May 1601, when the local people placed all their goods and cattle in the precinct, 'as in a santuarie.' The modern local place-names, Cnoc na Croise Mór (knoll of the large cross) and Cnocan na Croise Beage (hillock of the small cross), suggest that this sanctuary area may have been marked by stone crosses. Tradition maintains that the school continued to function until the eighteenth century. At the beginning of the ninteenth century the inside of the church was still decorated with sculpture, and the east gable supported a spire, or some would say a niche, decorated with three heads. Most of the freestone, however, including the altar, was subsequently removed.

Today the church is little more than a crumbling shell, measuring some 6.5 by 18.75 m, with walls 1.1 m thick standing in places up to 6 m high. It is built in rubble masonry, brought up to level courses; the western half of the building shows signs of having been built between timber shuttering, the tie-beams (or putlogs) of which have

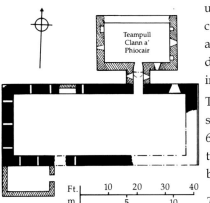

Teampall na Trionaid, Carinish (N. Uist), plan.

43

Teampall na Trionaid, Carinish (N. Uist).

left a series of small square holes piercing the wall where they have rotted away. The only architectural feature is a much-eroded lancet window near the east end of the north wall. While this might support a thirteenth-century date, it could equally well be as late as early sixteenth century.

On the north side of the church stand the remains of a smaller rectangular structure with steeply pitched gables which evidently once supported a timber roof. The east wall contains a splayed lintelled window flanked by wall-cupboards, and the west a single window and cupboard. The building is evidently later than the church, and was subsequently linked to it by a barrel-vaulted passage. Although its position is a normal one for a sacristy, the domestic character of the structure suggests a more plausible interpretation as a priest's house. Its modern name, Teampall Clann a' Phiocair (Chapel of the MacVicars), probably dates from post-Reformation times, when it was used as a family burial place.

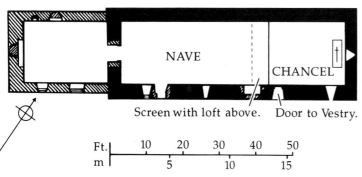

Eaglais na h-Aoidhe (St Columba's Church), Aignish (Lewis): plan.

10. Eaglais na h-Aoidhe (St Columba's Church), Aignish, Uidh (Lewis)

Located at the sea edge on the north side of the old cemetery of Aignish, signposted from the A866 (NB 485322). Access by track over machair land from roadside parking area.

Local tradition holds that the church of St Columba occupies the site of a cell of St Catan, who lived in the sixth and seventh centuries. The architecture of the present church, however, appears to be no earlier than fourteenth century. Margaret, the daughter of Ruairi, chief of the MacLeods of Lewis, was buried in the chancel area in 1503. In 1506 the rector was John MacLeod, and in 1534 and 1536 Sir Magnus Vaus. Martin Martin, in 1695, records the church's dedication as being to St Collum (or Columba); as one of the two parishes of Lewis, Uidh had a minister, though by this time the principal church would probably have been in Stornoway.

St Columba's church is an elongated rectangle in plan, measuring some 20.5 by 7 m overall, and facing north-east. It is built in rubble masonry, utilising the local gneiss, to which a red sandstone is added in later works. A slight discernible difference in the construction of the eastern third, corresponding to the chancel area, probably represents different campaigns of work, rather than different periods; it may in any case be more apparent than real, being emphasised by the plaster which still adheres to much of the chancel walls. More certain is the evidence for the heightening or rebuilding of the upper part of the north wall, probably as part of a re-roofing operation. This may have occurred in the sixteenth century, and have been contemporary with the addition of a burial mausoleum to the west end of the church.

The present door into the church is near the west end of the south wall; the original may possibly have been in the west gable. The point of division of the nave from the chancel, still clearly visible, was evidently originally marked by a timber screen with a loft above it, of which three supporting pockets for joists may be seen in north and south walls respectively. There is also a small window for lighting the loft on the south, and what appears to have been a larger window (now blocked)

below it, possibly for lighting an altar. Just inside the chancel, a narrow pointed-arched door in the south wall, opening outwards, probably led to a sacristy (now-demolished). The altar, placed against the east wall, would have been lit by a lancet window in the south wall and in the east wall behind it, though the pointed head of the latter has subsequently been replaced by a lintel.

The chancel was used in the fifteenth and early

Eaglais na h-Aoidhe (St Columba's Church), Aignish (Lewis), from S.

sixteenth centuries as a burial place for the MacLeods of Lewis and their families. Two grave-slabs have now been set up against the walls. On the south is a slab showing a male figure wearing a long quilted coat, a camail of mail around his neck and shoulders, and a pointed helm on his head. His left hand holds a sword. The man's identity is unknown, though it is possible that he was Roderick (Ruairi) MacLeod of Lewis, who died around 1498. The second slab is fixed to the north wall, and shows an interlaced cross, with various animals in the foliage. An inscription around the margin reads:

+ HIC . IACET /. MARGARETA . FILIA . RODERICI . MEIC . LEOYD ./ [DE . LEODHUIS . VIDUA . LACHLA]NNI . MEIC . FINGEO[NE . OBIIT .] M°V°III

Here lies Margaret, daughter of Roderic MacLeod of Lewis, widow of Lachlan MacKinnon. She died in 1503.

The burial aisle added to the west end of the church has a low arch in its west wall, evidently intended to contain a principal tomb, and was lit by broad rounded-arched windows on three sides; access to it was by a rounded-arched door in the south wall, or by another slapped through the west wall of the nave. The cemetery in which the church stands continues to suffer erosion by the sea and at one time extended much further north.

(top) Eaglais na h-Aoidhe (St Columba's Church), Aignish (Lewis): chancel
(left) Eaglais na h-Aoidhe (St Columba's Church), Aignish (Lewis): tomb, possibly of Roderick MacLeod (d.1498).

11. Teampall Mholuaidh (St Molua's Church), Eoropie (Lewis)

Located 100 m N of road, accessible by path over crofting land (NB 519652). Owned by the Episcopal Church of Scotland, and always open.

St Moluag (or Molua) was an Irish saint, probably of mythical origin, whose cult is also found in medieval Scotland. Historical evidence for the foundation of his church at Eoropie, however, is entirely lacking.

The earliest reference appears to be that made by Martin Martin in 1695. He records that within living memory a pagan fertility ceremony, involving the sea-god, Shony, had been performed annually, at All Saints: 'The Inhabitants round the Island came to the Church of *St. Mulvay*, having each Man his Provision along with him; every Family furnish'd a Peck of Malt, and this was brew'd into Ale: one of their number was pick'd out to wade into the Sea up to the middle, and carrying

a Cup of Ale in his hand, standing still in that posture, cry'd out with a loud Voice, saying, *Shony, I give you this Cup of Ale, hoping that you'll be so kind as to send us plenty of Sea-ware, for inriching our Ground the ensuing Year:* and so threw the Cup into the Sea. This was perform'd in the Night-time. At his Return to Land, they all went to Church, where there was a Candle burning upon the Altar; and then standing silent for a little time, one of them gave a Signal, at which the Candle was put out, and immediately all of them went out to the Fields, where they fell a drinking their Ale, and spent the remainder of the Night in Dancing and Singing, *&c.*' A stop was eventually put to this practice, however, by the Protestant ministers of Lewis.

By the mid-nineteenth century, the church was abandoned and roofless, though its walls were relatively intact. It was restored and re-roofed by the architect J.S. Richardson in 1912.

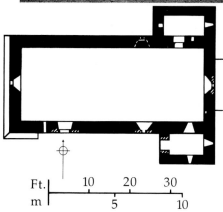

Ft. 10   20   30
m   5   10

(top) Teampall Mholuaidh (St Molua's Church), Europie (Lewis): from SW.
(left) Teampall Mholuaidh (St Molua's Church), Europie (Lewis): plan.

The church has a singular T-shaped plan, consisting of a rectangular nave-and-chancel, measuring some 7 by 15 m over walls 0.84 m thick, with a small sacristy flanking the north side of the chancel and a corresponding chapel the south. The roof over the main church is double-pitched, while those of the side-chambers are sloping. The door, with rounded arch and internal splay, is located towards the west end of the south wall. Narrow rounded-arched windows with external chamfers and internal splays are set in the gables and side walls, that on the east, behind the altar, having a pointed rear-arch. The chancel area is also lit by rectangular clearstorey windows above the roofs of the side-chambers. There is no longer any obvious division between nave and chancel, though the position of a former timber screen may be indicated by recesses just east of the north and south nave windows.

The sacristy is entered through a low door in the north side of the chancel; it has a slit window on the east, and niches, perhaps for lamps, on the west and south. Access to the south chapel is only possible from outside, through a door in its west wall; from it a squint window gave sight of the high altar.

The layout of the church has been compared to that of the Norse church at Gardar, in Greenland, where in the thirteenth century similar side-chambers were added to an existing twelfth-century building. However, excavations at Eoropie in 1977 demonstrated that the side-chambers were of one build with the nave. Although the period of construction has yet to be firmly established, the window details and battered wall base are echoed at St Clement's Church, Rodel, suggesting a date in the early sixteenth century.

12. Tur Chliamainn (St Clement's Church), Rodel (Harris)

In the care of Historic Scotland and always open (if locked, key obtainable from the hotel) (NG 048832).

According to Donald Monro, archdeacon of the Isles, who travelled through the Western Isles in 1549, the church of Rodel had been built by MacLeod of Harris. No doubt, Monro was referring to Alexander MacLeod of Dunvegan and Harris, otherwise known as Alasdair Crotach (or 'humpback'), whose tomb occupies a prestigious position on the south side of the choir. MacLeod died between 1545 and 1547; but the date 1528 given on his tomb indicates that the eastern part of the church had already been completed by then. Before his death, he was probably succeeded as clan leader by his son William, who in 1539 also prepared a tomb for himself in the south wall of the nave, where he was apparently laid to rest in September 1551. At least one of the transepts had probably been added by 1540, when David John McPersoun is mentioned as chaplain of St Columba's altar. On this evidence, the building may be dated between *c*.1520 and *c*.1540.

Although Monro described Rodel church as a 'monastery with ane steipill', there is no evidence that it was ever served by a monastic community: 'monastery' in this context probably means no more than a large and important parish church, what in England would be called a 'minster'. Nor is there any certain evidence for any earlier, Celtic church having occupied the site. Indeed, the dedication to St Clement, the third bishop of Rome after St Peter, who was martyred in AD 99, is quite consistent with a date after the Norse settlement; for Clement was much favoured as a patron of churches in the medieval Norse world. None the less, the church was indeed large by Hebridean standards, being exceeded in size only by the Benedictine abbey church on Iona itself.

The life of the church as a place of worship would have been short, for it appears to have gone out of use at the Reformation. The churchyard continued to be used for burials, but by the eighteenth century the church itself was roofless. A new roof was provided in 1784 by Captain Alexander MacLeod of Berneray, but no sooner was the work complete than it caught fire and burnt down,

Tur Chliamainn (St Clement's Church), Rodel (Harris): from SE.

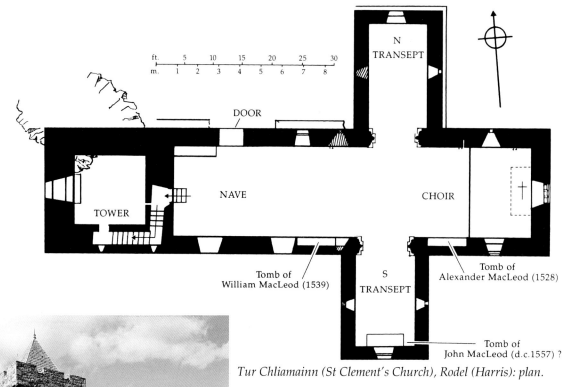

ft.   5   10   15   20   25   30
m.   1   2   3   4   5   6   7   8

N
TRANSEPT

DOOR

NAVE

CHOIR

TOWER

S
TRANSEPT

Tomb of
William MacLeod (1539)

Tomb of
Alexander MacLeod (1528)

Tomb of
John MacLeod (d.c.1557) ?

Tur Chliamainn (St Clement's Church), Rodel (Harris): plan.

with the result that it had to be restored for a second time in 1787 (as the inscription on the north wall of the nave tells us). By 1841, however, the church was again in a dilapidated condition. In 1873 it was restored once more by the architect Alexander Ross for the dowager countess of Dunmore.

The church is constructed in rubble masonry, with schist and freestone used for the finer dressings, the latter possibly imported from Mull. It is cruciform in plan, with a high rectangular tower at the west end, which, because of the sloping terrain, is entered from the west at a higher level than the rest of the church.

Tur Chliamainn (St Clement's Church), Rodel (Harris): tower from SW.

Seen from the outside, the tower is the dominating element and is elaborately decorated. It is four storeys high, and capped by battlements (rebuilt in the 1780s) and a pyramidal roof (of 1873). The windows are lancets with cusped heads. Between the third and fourth storeys, bull's heads project from the corners. Below these, half-way up, a cable-moulded stringcourse runs around the tower, stepping up at the corners, and at the centre of each face enclosing a sculpted panel: on the west, above the door, the figure of a bishop, probably St Clement, within a canopied niche; on the east, a much-worn representation of two fishermen in a boat, perhaps St Peter and St Andrew; on the north, a bull's head; and on the south, a nude female figure nursing a child and crouching to display her genitalia. The latter, though perhaps an unlikely ornament for a Christian church, belongs to a family of such late medieval female effigies, known as *Sheela na gigs*, that are found throughout Ireland and in those parts of Britain open to Irish influence. Although their origin was probably ancient, and rooted in paganism, their function by this period was benign, intended to ward off evil. Thus a sister of the Rodel *Sheela* is to be found in the outer wall of the Augustinian nunnery on Iona. Unusually, she also has a brother, who exhibits himself on the west face of the tower below the bishop's feet. This panel was apparently moved here from the parapet during restoration in the 1780s, together with another representing a second male figure, more seemingly attired in a kilt.

The church is entered through a door in the north wall of the nave, over which is a panel representing the crucifixion. The interior consists of a long rectangular space, some 18.6 by 4.9 m,

enclosed by an open timber roof dating from 1873. The windows comprise both slits and larger rectangular openings, the latter being mostly reworkings of the 1780s.

Originally the choir and sanctuary, which contained the high altar, would probably have been separated from the nave by a timber screen. But although there is no longer any trace of this, nor of the altar or clergy seats, the liturgical importance of the east end is still emphasised by its fine window of three lights with trefoil

Tur Chliamainn (St Clement's Church), Rodel (Harris): interior of nave looking W.

heads, surmounted by a spoked wheel enclosed by a pointed arch. Three surviving corbels projecting from the sanctuary walls suggest that in the 1784 restoration this was the location of the laird's loft; the focus of the church would then have been a timber pulpit (which has now gone), erected against the north wall of the nave in front of a blocked earlier window.

In the south side of the choir, before the sanctuary step, is the tomb of the founder, Alexander MacLeod, set within an arched recess covered by a low pediment. It comprises the finest ensemble of late medieval sculpture to survive anywhere in the Western Isles. A stone effigy of the dead man, dressed in plate armour and guarded by crouching lions, lies on top of the chest that was to contain his mortal remains. The sculptor has chosen to take the arch that encloses the tomb as symbolising the arc of the firmament, with God the Father holding the crucified Christ at its apex. The Holy Spirit, shown as a dove, may once have occupied a position at the foot of the cross. This representation of the Trinity is surrounded by symbols of the four evangelists, and flanked by the twelve apostles (with St Paul replacing Judas), and two angels with censers. Below the arch is the sun, flanked by a pair of angels blowing trumpets and holding two lighted candles. In the register

below this, the saints, through whom mortals approach God, are respresented by the Virgin Mary, flanked by two bishops wearing mitres and holding croziers, one of whom, holding a skull, is identified by an inscription as St Clement, the patron of the church. These figures are flanked in turn by symbols of the MacLeod clan, from whom the dead man was descended: on the left, a castle, probably Dunvegan in Skye, and to the right a galley under sail. The world of living mortals is represented in the bottom register by a hunting scene, in which two stags are pursued, at a sedate pace, by a knight wearing a pointed helmet and a coat of mail, accompanied by two gillies with dogs. To the right of this, St Michael and Satan weigh the souls of the

Tur Chliamainn (St Clement's Church), Rodel (Harris): tomb of Alexander MacLeod.

departed, to determine who should ascend to the Father and who descend to hell. Next comes an inscription, in poor Latin, recording:

+ *HIC . LOCULUS . CO(M)POSUIT*
PER D(OMI)N(U)M . ALLEXA(N)DER . FILIUS . VIL(EL)MI
MAC . CLOD . D(OMI)NO . DE DU(N)BEGAN
ANNO . D(OMI)NI . M.CCCCC.XXVIII

+ *This tomb was prepared*
by Lord Alexander, son of William
MacLeod, lord of Dunvegan,
in the year of Our Lord 1528

Additional chapels were provided in the transepts which flank the nave to north and south. Although these are irregularly disposed and the arches separating them from the nave differ, the northern one being rounded and constructed in schist, the southern one pointed and of freestone, the mouldings are similar and apparently of roughly the same date. A tomb located in the south transept may be that of John MacLeod of Minigish, William's successor as clan leader, who died around 1557. His effigy is represented in plate armour, with a conical helmet and with lions crouching at his head and feet.

Tur Chliamainn (St Clement's Church), Rodel (Harris): view from N transept to S transept

The north transept contains a collection of graveslabs which formerly covered tombs in the floor of the sanctuary. Four date from the early sixteenth century, and show a sword enclosed by patterns of interlace, while the fifth is dated 1725.

Against the north wall of the nave is the tomb of William MacLeod of Harris, son of Alasdair Crotach, who died in September 1551. The tomb-recess is enclosed by a semi-circular arch, above which is a triangular label moulding containing in the tympanum a panel showing the crucified Christ, with St Mary and St John. The effigy of the dead man is attired in plate armour and a pointed helm, his feet resting on two dogs, with another pair flanking his head. An inscription on the back wall could at one time be read as follows:

+ HI[C . E]ST . LOCULU[S . CO(M)P]OSUIT P(ER)
. D(OMI)N(U)[M . VIL(EL)MUM . MAC . LOD]
[A]NNO . D(OMI)NI . M[.CCCC]C.XX[XI]X

+ *This is the tomb prepared by*
Lord [William MacLeod]
in the year of Our Lord 1539

Further down the nave, in the south-west window opening is displayed the head of a late medieval disc-headed cross, which at one time would have stood outside the church. The front shows the crucifixion, while interlace decorates the reverse. A door at the west end of the nave leads up a narrow passage and steps into the ground floor of the tower, from which a series of ladders give access to the upper floors.

The Western Isles are a unique area in which visitors can study a complete range of housing types, from indigenous beehive cells and chimneyless, windowless byre-dwellings, through masonry, mass-concrete, corrugated iron, timber and precast concrete houses, to present-day 'kit-housing'. Many of the earlier types of building are no longer inhabited, and survive now as archaeological monuments in the landscape.

The Great Rebuilding in England took place in the seventeenth century, but Scots law delayed this process north of the border for almost a century. As a result, Scottish housing was largely 'unimproved' at the time of the 1745 rebellion. The subsequent opening up of the Highlands by the construction of military roads set the scene for improvement, but the low rental value of the small farms and crofts of the Highlands and Islands prevented the process from affecting those areas by up to another century and a half. As a result, indigenous housing was still being occupied well into the present century.

Although the eighteenth- and nineteenth-century improvers saw the new-style housing and agriculture as a positive step forward and a way of 'civilising' the inhabitants, recent research has shown that the principles behind the indigenous forms were more soundly based and 'environmentally friendly' than those of the 'improved' houses that replaced them. The pre-improvement houses of the Hebrides were described by Dr Samuel Johnson in 1773:

> The inhabitations of men in the Hebrides may be distinguished into huts and houses. By a HOUSE, I mean a building with one storey over another; by a HUT, a dwelling with only one floor. The laird, who formerly lived in a castle now lives in a house; sometimes sufficiently neat, but seldom very spacious or splendid ... Huts are of many graduations: from murky dens, to commodious dwellings. The wall of a common hut is always built without mortar, by a skilful adaptation of loose stones. Sometimes perhaps a double wall of stones is raised, and the intermediate space filled with earth. The air is thus completely excluded. Some walls are, I think, formed of turfs, held together by wattle, or texture of twigs. Of the meanest huts, the first

room is lighted by the entrance, and the second by the smoke-hole. The fire is usually made in the middle. But there are huts, or dwellings of only one storey, inhabited by gentlemen, which have walls cemented with mortar, glass windows, and boarded floors. Of these all have chimneys, and some chimneys have grates.

The house and the furniture are not always nicely suited. We were driven once, by missing a passage, to the hut of a gentleman, where, after a very liberal supper, when I was conducted to my chamber, I found an elegant bed of Indian cotton spread with fine sheets. The accommodation was flattering: I undressed myself, and felt my feet in the mire. The bed stood on the bare earth, which a long course of rain had softened to a puddle ... The petty tenants, and labouring peasants, live in miserable cabins, which afford them little more than a shelter from the storms.

Johnson was reasonably fair in his assessment, unlike many later travellers who measured the local housing conditions unfairly against the elegance of a Georgian mansion, without considering the difference in running costs. However, some writers did recognise the suitability of the Hebridean houses, and the Board of Agriculture reporter for the county of Inverness in 1808 stated:

Returning again to the treeless islands ... we have to notice that almost to the present time the dwellings of those people who had made least change to their mode of life could scarcely be more suitably constructed if their climate was one of continuous frost. With a long preceding passage or chambered porch leading to a low and narrow door, itself almost the only communication with the external air – with walls out of all proportion, thick for protection from the weather or support to the roof – the floor partially sunk – no vent in the roof but one or two insignificant light-holes in the eaves – an oven-like recess for the dormitory of the family – the cattle in the same apartment as the people, and with the fermenting refuse lying undisturbed throughout the winter, there could scarcely be a more effectual means used for keeping out the cold.

Many of the early townships were cleared in the nineteenth century, just as those in the Lowlands, and new enclosed farms were set up, with two-storey farmhouses and stone-built steadings. These, according to John Claudius Loudon in 1831, were 'tolerably decent,' built of stone and lime, and roofed with blue slates. He predicted that should this order of farmers survive for a further half-century, their houses would be as commodious and their steadings as well planned as those of the same class of farmer in any part of Britain. This type of house can be seen in many of the townships of South Uist in particular, but in most cases the new farm was eventually broken up and returned to the crofting system, with a planned township of thatched houses superimposed over the improved farm layout. The farmhouses, in these cases, were subdivided to accommodate crofters.

Captain F.W.L. Thomas, RN, was one of the first to recognise the archaeological implications of the indigenous dwellings:

> It is in the west of Lewis we meet with the dwellings having peculiar archaeological characteristics: the walls, rounded at the angles, are from 5 feet to 7 feet [1.5-2.1 m] in thickness, or they may be considered as two walls, with the interspace filled with rubbish; and the effect of this great thickness is that the roof rests on the inner edge, leaving a broad terrace on the top ... Externally, there is no smoke hole or window; but the purpose of both is served by two holes, about a foot [0.3 m] square, in and at the bottom of the thatch ...

> The outer door opens upon the fosgalan or porch, which is a small oblong, 12 feet by 6 feet [3.7 by 1.8 m], and in which there is often a quern (bra) upon a fixed board. The horse is accommodated here in severe weather; and as he almost fills the place, it is sometimes difficult to get past him ... A door from the fosgalan leads into the main building, which is entirely open through its whole length. In the present example [see illustration] the dimensions are 30 feet by 13 feet [9 by 4 m], but the length is often much greater, when they have a truly cavernous appearance. If the sun is shining brightly, the cottages appear on entering to be quite dark ... About two-thirds of the lower end is occupied by cows; the upper or fire-end is marked off by a row of stones (stall) 6 or 8 inches [15–20 cm] high. The fire, which never goes out, is about the middle of the floor; on the right-hand side is a bench of wood, stone or turf on

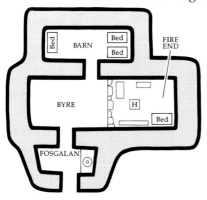

which the men sit; on the opposite side the women perform their domestic duties. Tables and chairs are almost unknown; but the evidently modern luxury of bedsteads and a dresser are quite unusual ... Behind the dresser is the calve's location, because it is near the fire; and the cows are tethered in winter along the wall ... A door opposite the entrance-door admits to the barn, which is also commonly a sleeping place of the grown-up young people.

Thomas also describes an older form of house at Valtos, Uig (Lewis), called a *creaga*. A pair of these houses that he described and illustrated still survives as a ruin below the broch at Carloway (Lewis). The first (A) was 'merely a long apartment, with a *cuil-ghast* (locked-end) or barn attached across the upper end.' The other house (B) had a *fosgalan* and a barn adjoining the side. Its main point of interest, however, was the presence of an oval-shaped bed-space (a) in the thickness of the wall at the upper end, measuring 76 cm wide at the head and narrowing towards the foot. Its cross-section was triangular, and the entrance hole was about 46 cm wide, and 61 cm from the floor. Thomas stressed that his examples were drawn from a limited area, and noted, 'much remains to be done in the way of excavating, planning, and measuring.' Unfortunately he was unheeded at the time, and this work is only now beginning to be done.

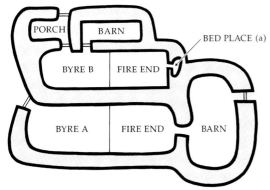

Plan of creaga ruin below Dun Carloway (Lewis), described by Capt Thomas RN.

The use of turf as a walling material appears to have been widespread, and is recalled by Joseph Mitchell, reminiscing in 1883 about his stay in Lewis. By this time the estates were attempting to change the situation. The *Rules and Regulations for the Lewis Estate in 1879* stipulated that the dwelling houses erected by the tenants should be 'of stone and lime, or of stone and clay pinned and harled with lime, or with stone on the outer face, and turf and sod on the inside, and roofed with slates, tiles, or straw, or heather with divots ... each house to have at least two apartments, with a glazed window in the wall of each, and a closet or small room with chimneys in the gables, or other opening for smoke in the roof; the thatch or covering not to be stripped off or removed for manure;

the byre to be built at the end or back of the dwelling house, as the site may admit, and to have a separate entrance. In the byre a gutter to be formed for manure, which shall be regularly removed to the dung heap outside.'

The term 'blackhouse' is confusing, as no two definitions seems to agree in all respects. It was first used officially in the report of the Royal Commission on the Housing of the Working Classes in 1885, when the prefix 'black' was taken to mean no more than 'inferior', in the same way that 'black-cattle' referred to unimproved breeds. The report of the Royal Commission on the Housing of the Industrial Population of Scotland: Rural and Urban, published in 1917, describes three different types of blackhouse. The 'old type', which had by then almost disappeared, had a single apartment, walls and roof-covering mostly of turf, and a smoke hole and a pane of glass for a window in the roof. The 'new type' contained one or two apartments; the entrance was through the byre, from which the living room was separated by a low mud-daubed partition, and the box-beds were screened off at the far end. The walls of the 'new type' were faced with stone; and the roof was more elaborately constructed and covered with straw thatch held down by stone-weighted heather ropes. The third or 'renovated type' contained three apartments, separated by timber partitions. The roof extended over the walls, which were usually reduced in thickness, provided with windows and a chimney in an end gable, and faced with mortar.

The same report describes the 'white house' as being similar to the contemporary cottar house of mainland Scotland, suggesting that it would also have been thatched, but symmetrical in layout with windows to either side of the doorway. Later on, the term 'white house' came to refer to other styles of dwelling, with the result that some confusion surrounds the use of the term today.

Walls of a house below Dun Carloway (Lewis)

Before local government reorganisation in 1975, the Western Isles were under the control of two mainland counties: Lewis was part of Ross and Cromarty, while Harris and the islands south of it belonged to Inverness-shire. The main differences in the housing stock surviving in these two areas stem from this division. The Ross and Cromarty sanitary inspectors of the turn of the century complained about the byre-dwellings and tried to change the situation gradually, but with very little success until after the 1917 Royal

Commission report. The Inverness-shire inspectors, on the other hand, took a much harder line, and began to take legal action to force change. The actions began about 1893, and by 1906 the report for Harris showed the total of 'good blackhouses' and 'white houses' marginally outnumbering 'bad blackhouses' and byre-dwellings ('cattle-housing').

Photographic evidence shows that the majority of rural houses were still thatched, and it is known that in the Uists thatched houses were still being erected in considerable numbers until the late 1920s, with one well-known example at Howbeg (South Uist) dating from 1938.

Other building materials were also being used. Corrugated iron was first patented in 1828, and was being mass-produced from the 1840s onwards. The date of its introduction into the Western Isles is not known, but Campbell of Jura bought prefabricated buildings to house his tenant farmers in 1853. These farmers moved directly from their turf dwellings into this new form of housing, occupying the iron buildings for about fifty years before they were

(top) Craigston (Barra), thatched house of the type dewscribed as a 'white house'
(left) Howbeg (S. Uist): thatched house of 1938.

replaced by 'traditional' stone dwellings. A similar history exists for the use of mass-concrete made with Portland cement. It was introduced into east-central Scotland in the 1820s and was adopted by the population of the Carse of Gowrie, who had a long tradition of using shuttered clay as a building material. By the 1870s, it was being used on the west coast of Scotland in Morvern parish, Lochaber. Again there is evidence of its use not only for modern white houses, but also for earlier forms of thatched houses. The

use of three-ply bituminous felt as a roofing material has an even earlier history, being first recorded at Greenock in the 1760s. It was made from sheething paper dipped in bitumen, dried, then re-dipped, and applied to the roof with 5 cm laps; the joints for the second and third layers were staggered one-third the width of the sheet in each case. This shows that there was no clear-cut progression, and that these 'modern' materials were available long before the Lewis Estate introduced their regulations requiring that new houses be stone-faced.

In addition to the housing of the townships, a large number of isolated 'shielings' may be observed in the inland upland areas of the Western Isles, where folk from the townships would pasture their sheep and cattle and cut peats during the summer months. A variety of structures is represented, from corbelled stone cells to timber and corrugated-iron shacks, some of which are still in use today.

Balgary (S. Uist), thatched house with mass-concrete chimney and thatch weighted down with rope.

The development of Stornoway

Stornoway is the only historic burgh in the Western Isles, and has a similar sequence of development to most other Scottish burghs. The earliest settlement was along a street corresponding to modern Point Street, which ran east-west along the spine of the natural promontory dividing the inner harbour from the outer, with the castle at its south-western tip (in the position now occupied by the ferry terminal). Tenement strips ran back at right angles from this street to terminate in the back lanes running along the north and south shores. Although the origins of this plan are uncertain, it is possible that they were formalised in 1598, when James VI settled a group of 'Gentlemen Adventurers' from Fife here, in an unsuccessful attempt to 'colonise' Lewis and exploit its agriculture and fisheries, in much the same way that was later attempted in Ireland.

In 1610 the Adventurers left, and the island was sold to Mackenzie of Kintail, whose descendents were the earls of Seaforth. During the seventeenth century, a number of Dutch fishermen settled in Stornoway, drawn there by the herring fisheries; and, in 1653, the castle was destroyed by Cromwell's forces, who constructed and briefly occupied a fort there.

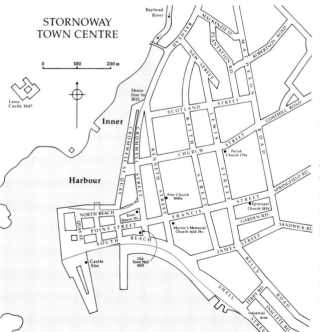

Because of the constraints of the site, the only possible direction in which the burgh could expand was towards the east. The principal streets, already shown on John Wood's map of 1821, were Dempster Street (today Cromwell Street), following the waterfront northward around the eastern edge of the inner harbour, and behind it Kenneth Street; both streets intersected Point Street at right angles. In 1844, Sir James Matheson purchased Lewis from the Seaforth Trustees, and a number of improvements were made. Matheson also constructed Lews Castle on the site of Seaforth Lodge, work beginning in 1847. To do this he cleared tenants

Stornoway, plan of the town centre.

from the grounds and enclosed an area of common grazing, much to the displeasure of the local inhabitants.

The suburban development of the late nineteenth and early twentieth century occupies the area east of the Georgian development, the whole being surrounded by modern housing schemes and bungalow suburbs. One area worth a visit is the late nineteenth- and early twentieth-century suburban villa development around Matheson Road, which, owing to difficulties of transport, still retains its pre-Second World War garden railings. All of the major Scottish foundries are represented, their names being cast into the designs.

Stornoway, railings in Matheson Road.

Post-Medieval sites and buildings to visit:

13. Hirta, township and field system (St Kilda)

The principal island in the St Kilda group, and a World Heritage Site, (NF 102993). In the ownership of the National Trust for Scotland, who manage it jointly with Scottish Natural Heritage. Intending visitors should contact the National Trust for Scotland for information on visits and accommodation. All visitors should report to the Scottish Natural Heritage warden on landing.

Although archaeological finds of the Iron Age, Early Christian and Viking periods have been found on Hirta, the archipelago only appears to have been permanently inhabited from the Middle Ages onwards. Most of the surviving structures, however, date from the nineteenth century. The original layout of fields and buildings on Hirta have still to be established, but it is known that the former strip field system was reallocated every three years.

The present village was set out in the 1830s, together with a new field system radiating from the bay in a fan shape. The line of

Hirta (St. Kilda), village

houses followed the contours, each house in the centre of its crofting strip. The 1830s houses were thatched and sat at right angles to the 'street'. The 1860s saw the erection of zinc-roofed stone-and-mortar-walled dwellings and the reuse of the 1830s houses as byres and stores. However, because the zinc roofs of the new houses tended to cause condensation, which rotted the timbers, after they were eventually blown off they were replaced with bituminous felt roofs, which lasted until the 1930s.

The church and manse were built in 1828 to a design by Robert Stevenson; and a schoolroom was added to the church in 1900. A two-storey storehouse was erected close to the shore to store the annual produce, consisting mostly of grain and sea-bird feathers, prior to shipping. The only other two-storey building was the factor's house. In addition to being used by the factor on his annual visit to collect the rents from the inhabitants, it provided accommodation for the school teacher, various visitors and, in this century, the district nurse.

Among a number of other types of structure represented on Hirta is a souterrain, in which sherds of Iron Age pottery have been found. The whole island is covered with corbelled stone structures known as 'cleits'. These are parallel-sided corbelled structures with rounded ends. The doorway is usually in the uphill end or in the side. Cleits were used for the storage of dried sea-birds, fish, hay and turf, but the sheer number of them appears out of all proportion to the population of 180 souls recorded from the late seventeenth century. The dried sea-birds were puffins, gannets and fulmars, which were harvested on a scale unknown elsewhere in Britain. There are also cleits on

other islands of the group, inclusing Boreray, Soay, Stac an Armin and Stac Lee.

A number of beehive cells clustered around what appear to be folds for animals may be seen at Gleann Mór. These are known to have been used as sheiling sites, but, like the corbelled buildings on Rona (see pages 22–5), may reflect an earlier lifestyle.

In the late seventeenth century the inhabitants numbered 180, but in the 1880s almost

Hirta (St Kilda), cleits.

half the population left for Australia. This was a major blow to the survival prospects of those who remained, and the island was eventually evacuated in August 1930.

The National Trust for Scotland took over the administration of St Kilda in 1957, and in the same year the Ministry of Defence established a base on Hirta for tracking missiles fired from the rocket-testing station on South Uist.

14. Arnol, blackhouse (Lewis)

Located in Arnol township at No. 42; signposted from the A858, with parking near by (NB 312491). In the care of Historic Scotland (admission charge).

The blackhouse at No. 42 Arnol is a very unusual monument, in that although it represents a type of building incorporating house and byre with a pedigree of at least a thousand years, it was constructed as late as 1885. The principles which lay behind the form and construction of the

indigenous Lewis blackhouse were sound and formed a direct response to the inhabitants' requirememts, modified by geographical location and the economics of the crofting system.

The plan derived from the need to maximise the shelter afforded by the croft buildings whilst utilising the heat given off by the livestock to supplement that from the peat fire. The family occupied one end of the principal range, the cattle the other. In the early houses this was a single volume, but later houses, including No. 42 Arnol, had timber partitions across the building which stopped short of the roof apex.

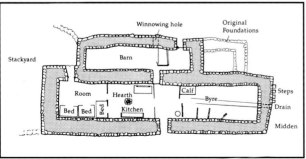

The byre was normally downhill of the dwelling space. In some townships there was a step down into it to allow dung to accumulate until it was required for the fields; but at Arnol there was no step, as the byre was cleared out daily. Houses in the adjoining townships also had an additional door in the byre gable, or a demountable turf gable, to allow

(top) Arnol (Lewis), blackhouse, from SW.
(left) Arnol (Lewis), plan of the blackhouse.

the dung to be removed using a garron (small horse) with panniers, slipe or cart. In all cases the byre drain ran out through the gable to a midden below the house.

Keeping cattle in a chimneyless space containing a fire presented problems, as cattle are susceptible to chest complaints. The problem was solved by giving the roof a distinctive shape. The area of roof over the house had a 45-degree pitch to contain the smoke pall. At the byre end, however, the roof pitch varied from 45 degrees where it joined the house, to 20 degrees at the bottom end. The resulting shape assisted the heat rising from the cattle to form a warm air curtain, preventing smoke penetrating the byre. This convection current of warm air also had a secondary effect, as it carried into the house a weak solution of ammonia in the water vapour given off from the cattle's urine. This ammonia tended to reduce cases of tuberculosis, a fact regularly commented upon in medical journals of the nineteenth century. Dairy maids were considered immune from the disease for the same reason. The doors into the principal range were at either side of the top end of the byre, again to assist in smoke control.

The barn ran parallel to the principal range, with a mutual wall between them, thus forming a porch on that side of the building (in the case of No. 42 Arnol, the north side). In some townships, there was a similar parallel range on the front of the house, used as a store and occasionally to stable a garron. These ranges had a standard pitch to the roof, though there was a rise in the mutual wall to allow the rainwater to drain away from the lintel of the connecting door.

The house end of No. 42 Arnol is divided into two by a timber partition. The first room contains the fire, set in the middle of the stone floor on a pad of baked clay, with a chain hanging above it for suspending a pot or kettle. This was the kitchen and principal living room. The roof over this part of the building has no turf below the straw thatch, so that the smoke can escape easily through it. Before it was restored in the 1970s, the walls of the room were decorated with wallpaper up to the level of the top of the partition. Furnishing is sparse, consisting of no more than a bench along one wall and a dresser, a cupboard and a chest of drawers on the other.

Arnol (Lewis), blackhouse: byre.

A door at the far end of the kitchen leads through a wooden partition into the bedroom. This contains three timber box-beds, one of which was entered directly from the kitchen. Before the 1970s restoration, the bedroom's walls were also coated with wall-paper; but here the paper ran across the undersides of the joists from wall to wall to form a ceiling and reduce the amount of smoke entering the sleeping area.

The house walls were made extremely thick for two important reasons. First, the fore-edge of the exposed wallhead acts as a wind-spoiler/deflector, preventing the wind from getting under the bottom of the thatch and stripping the roof. Second, and probably more significantly, the exposed wallhead provides a platform for repairing the thatch; however, the wallhead is susceptible to damage if walked on regularly.

There were several reasons for building a house without a chimney. The dead smoke in the roof space tends to extinguish sparks from the fire; it coats the timbers with tar, which helps their preservation; it prevents fungal growth in the thatch, turf, and timbers; it discourages insects such as midges and mosquitoes, wood borers, houseflies and other species that might contaminate food. Meat and fish could also be dried and smoked by hanging them from the roof timbers, and the soot-laden thatch made an excellent top dressing for the potato crop.

Originally blackhouses had wattle doors similar to many Irish houses. This helped to control the smoke between the house and byre. Later doors were made of planks and hinged rather than wedged in place. No. 42 Arnol probably always had plank doors, but whatever the type it was essential that they were not tight-fitting, as a certain amount of draught was necessary to keep the fire burning overnight and to prevent the occupants from suffocating. The drainage holes at the lower end of the byre also assisted with ventilation.

The rounded form of the roof was a direct result of the thatching technique. The straw was applied without any form of fixing, and was teased out and sprinkled on the roof before being compressed; no attempt was made to to align the stems in any particular direction. Only after the whole roof had been covered was a net applied

Arnol (Lewis), blackhouse: house end.

and the entire roof weighted down with stones and ropes. The thatch worked in the same way as on a potato clamp. Warm damp air rose from the interior to meet rain penetrating from outside. The moisture was then passed to either side of the roof, travelling along short lengths of straw in a similar way to traditional thatched roofs. Thatching was normally a community activity, and the larger the workforce available, the faster and easier the work proceeded.

Thatched roofs required continual maintenance and a constant source of heat such as a fire or a cattle byre beneath them. Once they were abandoned, or even left uninhabited for long periods of the year, they soon fell into decay; and when the roof decayed, the rest of the building quickly followed suit. A large number of ruined blackhouses may still be seen throughout Arnol township and elsewhere in Lewis; but without the surviving example at No. 42, it would be hard to imagine what they were originally like, or to appreciate the sophistication of their design.

Arnol (Lewis), township from the air, showing ruined blackhouses.

15. Garenin, township and blackhouses (Lewis)

Signposted from the A858 at Carloway (NB 192442). In the care of Comhairle nan Eilean and Urras nan Gearranan (The Gearranan Trust)

The building ruins, field boundaries and crofting strips are set on gently sloping ground, making the relationships easy to appreciate. Some of the ruined blackhouses are presently being restored by Urras nan Gearran. Some will be restored to their original condition, while others will be adapted to modern-day requirements for holiday accommodation, catering and a crofting environmental centre.

16. Shawbost, grain mill (Muilinn nan Gobharchean)(Lewis)

Approached by footpath 900 m over the moor from a carpark beside the A858 (NB 244464). In the care of the Shawbost Norse Mill Society.

The building was known as the Mill of the Blacksmiths and has been reconstructed. It has a roughly oval plan, and straddles the mill race. The upper chamber contains the mill stones, the lower the horizontal water-wheel.

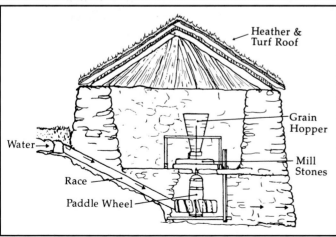

Water for the mill came from the burn that flows from Loch Raoinavat (beside the carpark) and continues past the mill into Loch na Muilna. The lade bringing water from the burn is formed of flat stones set in clay to make it watertight. The final section, the 'race', is lined with timber and steeply angled to direct the maximum power on to the paddles of the wheel. This is set horizontally, with a vertical drive shaft rising from it to the upper millstone. The height of the cut was adjusted by jacking up the beam under the drive shaft. A trip system on the upper stone shakes a hopper, which discharges the grain into a hole in the centre of the mill stone. After passing between the stones, the shelled grain or finished meal was then contained by the concrete kerb, to allow it to be collected without waste.

The reconstruction has a double-skin wall, yet photographs of other horizontal mills in the adjoining townships of Bragar and Arnol show that they had an inner skin of stonework and an outer one of turf.

These mills were once common throughout the Western Isles, and a number of ruined examples can still be seen on the edge of burns. Similar mills are also found in Orkney and Shetland. Although they are often referred to as 'Norse mills', there is nothing exclusively Scandinavian about them, for pre-Viking examples have been excavated in Ireland and the type was once common throughout Europe. They were eventually superseded by estate mills, which are similar to the meal mills found throughout Scotland.

17. Bunavoneadar, whaling station (Harris)

The site is signposted from the junction of the A859 and B887 (NB 131039). In private ownership.

The site of the former whaling station lies at the head of West Loch, in a small inlet known as Bun Abhainn-eadar. Most of the buildings have now been demolished to their foundations, the only structure surviving relatively intact being the chimney of the dessicator.

Whaling in North Harris began in 1895, and by 1907 Captain Carl F. Herlofsen established a permanent base at Bunavoneadar. The site was licensed in 1907, when the Whale Fisheries (Scotland) Act was passed.

The whaling season ran from April to October, and the 90-foot (27.4 m) catcher ships worked as far north as Faroe to a few miles south of Barra Head, the main catching area being centred on Rockall, St Kilda and the Flannan Islands. The catch comprised Common Rorqual, Blue, Biscayan, Nordkaper's

and Sperm Whales, and less significant numbers of Humpback and Bottlenose. The fishing stopped during the 1914–18 war, but continued afterwards. Lord Leverhulme purchased the fleet from the Norwegians in 1922, carried out repairs to the station and added a laboratory. His fishery employed three catcher ships. A building to smoke whalemeat for sale in the Congo was added to the station just before it closed in 1929 on Lord Leverhulme's death. During Leverhulme's ownership the station processed 6,000 tons of whalemeat.

Bunavoneadar (Harris), whaling station, looking from the slipway towards the dessicator chimney.

The whales were towed into the bay and drawn up the slipway, where the blubber and baleen were removed. The carcase was moved to the side of the platform and the flesh stripped from the bones. It was placed in buckets and transferred to the boiling house. After boiling, the meat was dried slowly, and then ground for sale as cattle feed and manure to the Scandinavian market.

18. Butt of Lewis, lighthouse (Lewis)

Accessible by road, signposted from Eoropie at the junction of the B8013 and the B8014 (NB 519665). Operated by the Northern Lighthouse Trust, and open at set times (information posted on gate).

The dangers of navigating around the rugged coasts of the Western Isles have given rise to the development of a significant class of monument in modern times: the lighthouse. The first project of the Northern Lighthouse Trust after its establishment by Act of Parliament in 1786 was the lighthouse on Eilean Glas, Scalpay (Harris). Owing to the difficulties of working on so remote a site, 21 m above sea level, it required two seasons of construction work before the fixed light, designed by Thomas Smith of Edinburgh, was finally exhibited on 10 October 1789. The light is now on display in the Royal Museum of Scotland, Edinburgh.

The brick-built lighthouse tower at the Butt of Lewis was constructed in 1862 to the designs of David and Thomas Stevenson. The Stevensons had a long association with the Northern Lighthouse Trust. Robert Stevenson had constructed the lighthouse on Berneray (Barra), in 1833, and his family partnership was later responsible for those at Arnish Point, Stornoway (Lewis), in 1853, Usinish (South Uist) in 1857, the Monarch Islands in 1864, Eilean Mór in the Flannan Islands in 1899, and Tiumpan Head on the Uidh Peninsula (Lewis) in 1900.

Where space permitted, as at the Butt of Lewis, a normal feature of such lighthouses was the associated accommodation block for the keepers. Because of its remoteness, the Flannan Isles lighthouse also had a shore station, containing accommodation for the keepers' families. This takes the form of a red-brick, two-storey double-gabled structure, set back from the A858 at Breasclete (Lewis).

The road to the Butt of Lewis lighthouse passes through the remains of an open field runrig system, which is possibly the best-preserved, easily accessible example in the Western Isles, the only comparable system being on Rona (see page 22).

Some further reading

General

Barber, J. *Innesgall: The Western Isles* (Edinburgh n.d.)

Gifford, J. *Highland and Islands*. The Buildings of Scotland (London 1992).

MacDonald, D. *Lewis: A History of the Island* (Edinburgh 1979).

MacKenzie, W.C. *Book of the Lews* (Paisley 1919).

Ritchie, G., and M. Harman. *Exploring Scotland's Heritage: Argyll and the Western Isles* (Edinburgh 1985).

Robson, M. *Rona: The Distant Island* (Stornoway 1991).

Royal Commission on Ancient and Historical Monuments & Constructions of Scotland. *Ninth Report with Inventory of Monuments and Constructions in the Outer Hebrides, Skye and the Small Isles* (Edinburgh 1928).

Prehistoric

Armit, I. (ed.). *Beyond the Brochs: Changing Perspectives on the Later Iron Age in Atlantic Scotland* (Edinburgh 1990).

Feachem, R.W. *Guide to Prehistoric Scotland*, 2nd edn (London 1977).

Henshall, A.S. *The Chambered Tombs of Scotland*, 2 vols. (Edinburgh 1963-72).

MacKie, E.W. The Origin and Development of the Broch and Wheelhouse Building Cultures of the Scottish Iron Age. *Proceedings of the Prehistoric Society*, 31 (1965), 93-146.

Ritchie, G. and A. *Scotland: Archaeology and Early History* (London 1981).

Early Christian and Medieval

Barber, J. Excavations at Teampull Mholuaidh ... 1977. *Proceedings of the Society of Antiquaries of Scotland*, 110 (1980), 530-533.

Crawford, B.E. *Scandinavian Scotland* (Leicester 1987).

Dunbar, J.G. Kisimul Castle, Isle of Barra. *Glasgow Archaeological Journal*, 5 (1978), 25-43.

Duncan, A.A.M., and A.L. Brown. Argyll and the Isles in the Earlier Middle Ages. *Proceedings of the Society of Antiquaries of Scotland*, 90 (1956-7), 192-220.

Lawson, B. *St Clement's Church at Rodel: A Harris Church in its Historical Setting* (Northton, Harris, 1991)

—— *St. Columba's Church at Aignish (The Church of the Ui): A Lewis Church in its Historical Setting* (Northton, Harris, 1991).

Maclean, L. (ed.) *The Middle Ages in the Highlands* (Inverness 1981).

Macquarie, A. *The Church of St. Finnbarr, Barra: A Short History*, 2nd edn (Droitwich 1989).

Megaw, B. Norsemen and Native in the Kingdom of the Isles. *Scottish Studies*, 20 (1976), 1-44.

Munro, J. and R.W. *Acts of the Lords of the Isles, 1336-1493*. Scottish History Society, 4th series, vol. 22 (Edinburgh 1986).

Nisbet, H., and R.A. Gailey. A Survey of the Antiquities of North Rona. *Archaeological Journal*, 117 (1960), 88-115.

Ponting, G. *A Mini-Guide to Eoropie Teampull* (Callanish 1982).

Post-Medieval

Cheape, H. Horizontal Grain Mills in Lewis. *Highland Vernacular Buildings* (Edinburgh 1989), pp. 71-89.

Fenton, A. *The Island Blackhouse and a Guide to 'The Blackhouse', No. 42, Arnol* (Edinburgh 1978).

—— and B. Walker. *The Rural Architecture of Scotland* (Edinburgh 1981).

Martin, M. *A Description of the Western Islands of Scotland*, 2nd edn (London 1716, repr. Edinburgh 1981).

Mechan, D., and B. Walker. Possible Byre-Dwelling at Borve, Berneray, Harris. *Vernacular Building*, 13 (1989), 23-33.

Quine, D.A. *St Kilda Portraits* (Frome 1988).

Small, A. (editor). *A St Kilda Handbook* (Dundee 1979, repr. Edinburgh 1986).

Stell, G., and M. Harman. *Buildings of St Kilda* (Edinburgh 1988).

Thomas, Capt F.L.W. On the primitive dwellings and hypogea of the Outer Hebrides. *Proceedings of the Society of Antiquaries of Scotland* (1867), 153–195.

Walker, B. Traditional Dwellings of the Uists. *Highland Vernacular Buildings* (Edinburgh 1989), 50-70.

—— Edited Notes on Hebridean Buildings from Åke Campbell's Field Notebooks of July 1948. *Vernacular Building*, 13 (Edinburgh 1989), 47-61.

Printed in Scotland for HMSO by C.C.No. 22926 6c 5/94